Introduction
weathervanes
Chairs -
Decorative arts -
pottery
glassware
Shimmel toys -
portraits & furniture -

Tapestries

IN THE SAME SERIES

Glass and Crystal vol. 1
Glass and Crystal vol. 2
Dutch Tiles
Jewelry
Lace
The Dutch Windmill
Aquarium Techniques vol. 1
Aquarium Techniques vol. 2
Orchids
Pottery
Carpets from the Orient

Translated from the
Dutch by Alexis Brown

TAPESTRIES

W. S. Sevensma

UNIVERSE BOOKS, Inc.
Publishers
New York

First Printing

Published in the United States of America by

UNIVERSE BOOKS, Inc.
381 Park Avenue South
New York, N.Y. 10016

Library of Congress Catalog Card Number: 65 – 24049

Printed in The Netherlands

Contents

	Preface	7
I	**Tapestry**	9
	1. The technique in principle	9
	2. The materials employed	21
	3. About the people who made the tapestries	27
	4. The border of the tapestry	31
II	**Tapestry to the Beginning of the Middle Ages**	33
III	**Tapestry in the Middle Ages**	38
IV	**Tapestry in the Sixteenth Century**	49
	1. Brussels and other centres in the Spanish Netherlands	49
	2. The Region along the Loire	53
V	**Tapestry in the Seventeenth Century**	55
	1. Paris and other centres in France	55
	2. Brussels	59
VI	**Tapestry in the Eighteenth Century**	60
	1. Paris	60
	2. Brussels	63
VII	**The Development of Tapestry in Germany, Italy, Spain, England, Scandinavia and Russia**	69
	Germany	71
	Italy	75
	Spain	76
	England	77
	Scandinavian Countries	81
	Russia	81
VIII	**Tapestry in the Netherlands**	82
	Middelburg	85
	Delft	85
	Gouda	88
	Utrecht	88
	Amsterdam	89
	Schoonhoven	89
	The Hague	90
	Haarlem	90

IX   **The Renaissance in the Present Century** . . .   91

X   **Favourite Subjects for Tapestries**   96
      In the Fourteenth and Fifteenth Centuries   96
      In the Sixteenth Century   99
      In the Seventeenth Century   103
      In the Eighteenth Century   105

      Bibliography   106

      Museums   107

      Photographs   109

      Drawings   110

Preface

This book was written primarily for those for whom the word 'gobelin' or tapestry immediately conjures up memories of holiday hours passed in the evocative silence of old buildings. They do not associate the draughty walls of gloomy castles directly and inexorably with hardboard panelling and paint to keep out the damp, but rather with lightly stirring tapestries that catch the draught and check it.

Old churches for them are not simply dark and musty, but full of quiet colours gently glowing from the walls. Museums for them hold treasures of beauty demanding devoted attention.

They will find in this book a modest guide to the appreciation of a subject which has so vividly captured their interest. This branch of the textile art has an interesting history, not only of sumptuous materials and high artistic skill, but also and above all a history involving human beings: the rich, who could afford to buy the works of art of which we speak; and the people who in making them sometimes worked more than a twelve-hour day, wearisomely adding stitch to stitch and thread to thread.

The art of tapestry, as it develops historically, gives an interesting picture of the origin, flowering and decline of the cultures from which it emerged. Derived in the first place from the ancient east, and requiring a particular combination of artistic ability and business sense, here in the west it reached a marvellous efflorescence.

These remarkable products combine in their simple warp-and-weft technique more than mere threads of wool and silk; the titles and exploits of famous princes become involved in the events which tapestry portrays. Many of these tapestries have made history, and deserve above all to be admired for their own sake, quite apart from their desirability as property. In other words, they call forth an idealistic attitude from the man who admires them. This of course does not imply that important public sales should be ignored, but this book is not primarily concerned with those products of the loom which are now readily obtainable from any establishment of modern arts and crafts.

Publisher and author have chiefly focussed attention on the

tapestries that originated in the Middle Ages and in subsequent centuries up to and including the eighteenth. Consequently, the contents of the book will be easily followed by all who have a broad general interest in the theme. The information has been kept within bounds, and a labyrinth of technicalities avoided. The plan precludes not only a comprehensive, but even, in point of fact, a thorough treatment of the subject. This is particularly true of data given on the subject-matter of the tapestries, where no more than a summary has been attempted, to guide the reader somewhat among the multiplicity of themes to be found there.

The writer has endeavoured to give some indication, by means of charts, of the geographical evolution of tapestries in Europe. However, the data as to present distribution is not always fully reliable, since the destruction caused in the last world war cannot yet be taken fully into account.

Those who set store by a comprehensive and thorough treatment will find that the titles of more extensive works have been listed.

Furthermore, the author is not unaware how difficult it is for teachers who give lessons on this subject in the technical education of girls, to encounter reference works suitable for their pupils. Perhaps they most of all will find this little book of service to them in their teaching.

If these pages serve to increase interest in tapestry, an important purpose will have been achieved.

W. S. SEVENSMA

I Tapestry

1. The technique in principle

Probably at some time you have had the chance of looking at a tapestry more closely than usual. You may have been in a museum at the time, or even in some modern building, since there too, in halls and on staircases, one may come across tapestries. But museum-piece or not, contemporary or old, you would have noticed even by examining them casually that there are great differences among such tapestries, not only in artistic merit but also from the viewpoint of technique.

The basic principles of this technique are as follows: on a warp – usually of wool but sometimes of linen thread – is laid a weft, usually of wool, in the simplest way to make the warp-thread wholly invisible (fig. 1). Starting from the left, the weft thread first passes in front of the even warp threads (i.e. in front of the second, fourth, sixth and so on) and behind the odd (first, third, fifth and so on). This we call the half weft. It is then brought back, from the right – this time in front of the odd and behind the even warp threads. Thus the so-called whole weft is laid, after which the next one can be made.

The technique has this much in common with true weaving – that, just like the weaver of a piece of cloth, the maker of a tapestry uses a system of warp and weft. The difference however is that the tapisser when working across the warp brings the weft no further than the part he happens to be working on at that moment, while the weaver, generally speaking, uses the whole

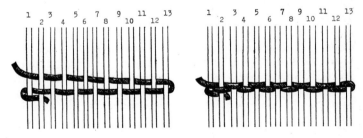

Fig. 1. Diagram of one whole weft.

9

breadth of the cloth for his weft, at each operation throwing the shuttle through the whole group of warp threads across the fabric, from one selvage to the other. In making a tapestry, however, each colour employed runs off a separate bobbin. Each shuttle is only used, therefore, when a particular colour is required.

This technique resembles embroidery in that the right colour can be introduced at the right place and in the right form, as desired. The difference here, however, is that the embroiderer works upon a piece of fabric that already exists, whereas the tapisser makes the fabric for himself as he goes along.

The principle which has to be grasped can only be called 'weaving' in a very special sense. People therefore have always tried to distinguish this craft from weaving by giving it a name of its own, though they have only been partly successful. The name *tapissier* arose in French (and from it, the English word tapisser) from *tapis*, a general name for stuffs suitable for draping on walls.

This lack of accepted terminology applies not only to the people who make tapestries, but also to the product itself.

The word tapestry, as we have already seen, says nothing particular about the technique, and so is much too generalised to be satisfactory. The name 'gobelin' though frequently heard is of no use unless closely defined, since by rights only one sort of tapestry ought to bear this name. Nor is the word *arrazzo*, formerly used by the Italians, or the English *arras*, any more acceptable, since each applies properly speaking only to a tapestry from Arras, which in former centuries was a famous centre of the craft. So for want of a better term we shall have to carry on with the one we know: tapestry, taking into account that it tells us nothing of the specific nature of the technique.

In making this sort of tapestry, weaving-looms of two kinds are used, but they are quite similar in principle. In the one, the warp is vertical; in the other, it lies horizontally. In English, these are known as high warp and low warp looms, respectively, while the Dutch employ the French expressions, *haute-lisse* and *basse-lisse*. Either style of loom occurs in a variety of sizes. Since, however, when talking of tapestries we usually bring first to mind the great wall-hangings often referred to simply as gobelins, the looms on which they were made will now be briefly described.

In the *haute-lisse* or high warp loom, two heavy, upright beams of timber are secured with the utmost solidity, preferably to roof and floor, and between them lie both the warp-beam and the cloth-beam – the former above, the latter below. Between these two beams, which in the larger looms are actually as thick as a tree-trunk, the warp threads are stretched. A groove or channel runs lengthwise along both beams, to contain a round rod to which the ends of the warp are fastened firmly. A heavy iron peg clamps this rod in the groove. Both beams are enormously thick, as they certainly need to be, for the tension of the warp threads exerted on the beam is very great – a pull of about $6\frac{1}{2}$ lbs on each separate thread.

In a large loom, assuming the space between the uprights (in other words, the length of the cross-beams) to be six yards, enabling a tapestry five yards wide to be made, the number of warp threads can safely be assessed as from three to four thousand. This number naturally depends on the thickness of the threads and their distance apart. The tension exerted by the threads is enormous. Using heavy levers to stretch the warp was, in former times, a risky business for those who did it, though later on, better methods were found. The ends of the cross-beams were attached to runners, which were moved up and down the heavy upright timbers by a sort of hoist, worked by cog-wheels. Thus the tension exerted on the warp could be regulated at need. The beams, however, were still shifted as seldom as possible, and with good reason.

As the weavers progressed with their task – on the big looms, sometimes five or more would be working next each other on one tapestry – they would reach the point where either the

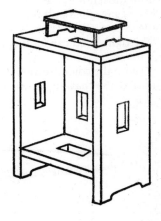

Fig. 2. Weaver's seat, with a small bench for extra height.

warp must be rolled further round the cloth-beam, or the weavers themselves must sit higher up, and this they did until the last possible moment. To meet this need a little bench was designed, of the right size for use in different positions (fig. 2).

In the *basse-lisse* or low warp loom, the whole frame, warp and all, lay horizontally, and the weaver sat at work directly behind the cloth-beam. The relative position of both cross-beams could be regulated by means of a screw-thread, so as to tighten or relax the warp. By means of a strong lever set in the frame, this type of loom could be turned, lifting the beams vertically at need, so the weaver might the better judge his work.

The weavers, as has already been briefly explained, had to insert their beechwood shuttles (fig. 3) alternately in front of one warp thread and behind the other. Consequently they were obliged to bring a certain number of warp threads simultaneously to the front, thus 'opening the fabric' as it was called.

A rounded stick or batten was used to make the opening, by so inserting it in the warp that odd and even threads were gathered into separate groups (fig. 4). Each weaver had such a batten for himself. Under the batten, cords were fastened in groups, by means of eyelets, to the odd and even threads respectively, and thence to rounded staves, hanging horizontally, so that one or other group of warp threads could be drawn to the front at will. These cords, or *lisses*, gave their name to the type of loom.

At the vertical loom, the weaver brings a group of odd threads forward simply by drawing them closer towards him with his left hand (fig. 5). His right hand now brings the shuttle from the left into the gap. The weaver, when he reaches the end of this gap, then pulls with his left hand on the cords attached to the even warp threads, so drawing the back group to the front. The right hand carries the shuttle back leftwards, so that a weft is made.

Once the colour section on which he happens to be working is finished, so that the shuttle with this colour is for the time being

Fig. 3. Beechwood shuttle for the high-warp loom.

12

Fig. 4. Cross-section showing the 'opening of the fabric' by means of the batten.

of no further use, then it is left hanging until the weaver needs to work in the same shade once more. Sometimes the thread is cut, leaving about 4 inches to be finished off later. Once laid, the weft is firmly pressed down first with the fingertips, then with the comb (fig. 6). Different combs are used, depending on the number of warp threads per inch.

In the horizontal loom the warp is opened by means of foot pedals (therefore known as *tapisserie à pédales*) with which the beams are connected. The width of the tapestry was divided into a number of working-widths, each of which has two beams – one for the even and one for the odd threads.

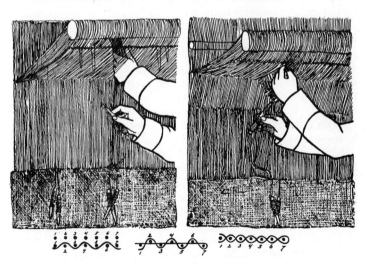

Fig. 5. The position of the weaver's hands when laying a half and a whole weft in succession.

Fig. 6. Comb used for pressing back the weft threads. Different combs were used, depending on the number of warp threads per inch.

Of these two looms, the vertical can perhaps be taken to be the older, and is represented in Ancient Egyptian and Greek art. However, the horizontal loom must have been in use for many centuries, as the Dutch word 'legwerker' applied to the working of this loom occurs in the archives at an early date.

Questions are frequently asked about the differences between the tapestries produced by these two looms, but they appear extremely difficult to discern, at least by our modern experts. Yet the rich patrons of former times seem to have been able to ascertain which technique had been used, when a piece of work was delivered to them. With the upright loom, the fabric must always be opened by hand, so that some of the threads will be pulled harder than others. This caused a difference in tension between the groups of warp threads, a difference that would be visible. The opening of the horizontal loom, however, was done by the feet in a uniform manner.

The worker at a high warp loom could only weave with one hand, whereas his colleague at the low warp loom had both hands free. No wonder that tapestries from the low warp loom could be produced more cheaply than from the upright. When profit was the first consideration, the horizontal loom was used for choice. Thus the greater part by far of the tapestries made during the course of the centuries was made on this loom.

With either sort of loom, the weaver starts off with nothing in front of him or below him other than a set of warp threads.

Has he a design to follow? Yes, certainly; before the weavers begin their part of the activity, a work-design is put either at the back of or underneath the warp, as the case may be. This design is made full size – the 'cartoon', so-called – a detailed plan of the whole work; sometimes painted in oils, sometimes in body colour.

The designers of these cartoons, for the most part nameless artists, are those who determined the distinctive style and high artistic value of the tapestries. True, they took directions from others – in the Middle Ages for example from the court painters

14

– but nevertheless the designers themselves rather than the court painters were the ones who determined the character of the tapestries, both in the Middle Ages and afterwards. Of course, they adopted their style from contemporary painting, yet still they managed to give it a particular expression, being obliged, because of the weaving technique, to adapt their designs accordingly.

Every part of the great whole, each leaf on a tree, must so to speak fulfil the requirements of the weaving technique. It could be said – we quote – that the painter in making the sketch provided the melody, and the designer of the cartoon added the orchestration. The latter, in consequence, was more highly paid. In the sixteenth century, it is true, the two came closer together, yet the cartoonist always kept an individual style.

In the seventeenth century, design began to deteriorate, as draughtsmen appeared who took only a specialised part of the overall theme in hand – one doing heads, another fruit, a third animals, and so forth.

But to return to the work-design itself. When in place, the workers draw round the design in coloured chalk, crossing over the warp threads, of course, as they do so. Thus a network of black or coloured points is formed, thanks to which the worker always has some guide to follow. After the pattern had thus been transferred to the warp, the design is left hanging on the wall, or left lying under the warp, in the case of the horizontal loom.

We ought here to make two observations. The first refers to the size of designs employed – how could they manipulate such enormous pieces of paper? One must bear in mind, however, that each weaver had only to copy his own section on to the warp. The complete design was therefore cut into long strips not more than about 12 inches wide. The second remark applies to the method of work that can be observed in Paris nowadays, at the very place, in fact, where the famous gobelins were made. There we may see that the weaver, with the help of a mirror, could at any moment he wished consult the design hanging behind him. In times gone by, however, this method was not known. Then, just as now, the weaver when he wanted to judge the effect of what he was doing, had to walk round to the other side of his piece of work. His work was done on the reverse side, for there hung the shuttles of unfinished thread, and the loose ends.

And here comes something else which doesn't exactly make it easy for the weaver. One must bear in mind that in this kind of work the warp is stretched between beams, as for ordinary fabric, yet that eventually, once the tapestry is finished, this warp will lie horizontally and not hang down vertically. In other words – the weft that the weavers insert crosswise in and out of a vertical warp will eventually hang down perpendicularly.

At this point, several queries arise. Employing this method, must an upright human figure, or a tree, or a wall, be worked in the fabric horizontally? For this reason, is not an assessment of the work during weaving almost impossible? Must not everything woven as if lying down be thought of as standing up? And – which sounds most peculiar – won't such a tapestry eventually be hanging by the weft threads? In fact, this is just what does happen. What is more, the weft threads are not continuous, since they only run to the edges of each colour section.

This simple fact accounts for the reason why these tapestries have offered such relatively little resistance to the inroads of time. The fatal flaw was just this business of hanging by the weft threads – a whole made up of little pieces. The very large and heavy tapestries commissioned in particular by the princes of Burgundy did not stay intact for long. Repairs were necessary after a few years, and in thirty years they were worn out.

There were of course other reasons besides. Many tapestries were moved from one residence to another – which meant being taken down and hung up again and again. Often they had to serve as decorative awnings in the streets, and were hung outside in the rain and the wind. Then too there were moths and mice, mould and damp – but hanging by the weft instead of the strong warp was undoubtedly the chief reason for their rapid disintegration.

The question of course now arises – why do it? Could not the same effect be achieved and yet have the fabric hung by the warp? Why make this trouble for oneself?

To answer these queries obliges us to go somewhat deeper into the technique of this remarkable sort of weaving. We have already seen how the design comes into existence by weft threads being laid on the heavy warp. Presently, the warp forms down the whole length of the tapestry the peculiar ribbing typical of these fabrics (fig. 7). The ribbing generally catches the light on one side, while the other side is in shadow. As far as he can, the weaver must use this to advantage. Now if

16

1. a and *b. Tapestry workshop, ateliers de la Savonnerie, showing work at the high-warp loom. c. Tapestry workshop, atelier de Beauvais Basse Lisse, showing the low-warp loom.*

2. *a. The Presentation in the Temple. Probably from the workshops of Nicolas de Bataille. Fourteenth century. b. Detail from the Miracle of St. Quentin (Cluny Museum). c. The Visitation, from a Gospel tapestry. Fifteenth century.*

3. *Norwegian folk-tapestry. Seventeenth century.*

4. Gobelin tapestries from the Manufacture royal de la Couronne. a. Louis XIV
laying the foundation stone of the Dome des Invalides. b. The finding of the
infant Moses.

5. a. Landscape woven in wool and silk. Paris, early seventeenth century, school of R. de la Planche. b. Roman centurion on horseback, with standard-bearers. Tapestry woven for the Mobilier National in Paris.

6. One of the Beauvais 'Grotesques'.

7. *The story of Abraham, Hagar and Ishmael. English tapestry, 1657 (Mort-lake).*

8. *a. Adonis killed by the wild boar. Mortlake, second half of the seventeenth century. b. Joseph recognised by his brothers. Woven by Neilson in 1773.*

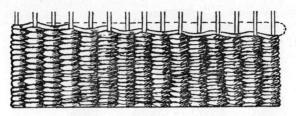

Fig. 7. The 'ribbing' characteristic of this sort of tapestry. The rib here is irregular, one side being higher than the other.

he lets the warp run perpendicularly through the fabric, instead of lying across, all this parallel ribbing would also run vertically through the main forms of his design – that is to say, through houses, trees, human figures, and so on.

And something else at least as important also arises, namely that the weaver is always obliged to keep each colour section on its own (fig. 8). When a particular colour is done with, the thread is snipped off or the spool is left hanging. The new thread of another colour is then laid: either on the same warp thread, above the last weft of the previous colour – so that at this spot there are two threads instead of the usual one (fig. 9) – or on the next warp thread, which means that at this spot the last warp thread within one colour, and the first warp thread within the following colour, have no link with each other. If this boundary between two adjacent colours runs along the same warp threads for many lines of weft, then a split will develop at that place (fig. 10).

Caucasian carpets that come on the market under the name of *kelim* show this method of work most clearly. They are made on the same principle as tapestries. Unlike *kelim* fabrics, however, the gaps in tapestries are, with a few exceptions, closed up later on, though sometimes they are left open, deliberately, to obtain the effect of shadow. When the tapestry comes to be hung, these splits of course lie horizontally, and then the fabric bulges out slightly, while the opening itself appears as a darker line. This, when outlining a profile, can be useful to mark the rounding of a chin, the tip of a nose, a kneecap, the tear-gland of an eye, etc. In Brussels especially, when the industry was in its heyday there, the craftsmen seem often to have employed these subtle tricks of the trade.

If we now ask ourselves what would be the result of hanging the warp vertically with the weft threaded across, it becomes

17

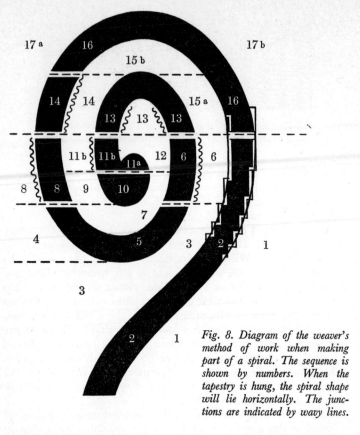

Fig. 8. Diagram of the weaver's method of work when making part of a spiral. The sequence is shown by numbers. When the tapestry is hung, the spiral shape will lie horizontally. The junctions are indicated by wavy lines.

plain that the splits too would run vertically. Thus, in the principal figures we mentioned just now, a large number of vertical chinks would appear, often taking up the greater part of the length of the tapestry (fig. 11). The colour-outlines of a fairly upright tree-trunk would well-nigh come loose from the surroundings.

Another consequence of the chosen method of work was that tapestries of almost unlimited width could be made. The length of the warp beams determined only the height of the tapestry. Specimens are known, six or seven yards high, that have attained a good twenty yards in breadth. The other method would require a loom more than twenty yards broad, which is of course impossible.

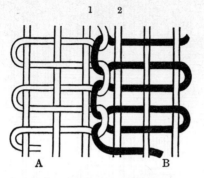

Fig. 9. The joining of two colour sections.
This junction occurs at the places shown
in fig. 8 by a wavy line.

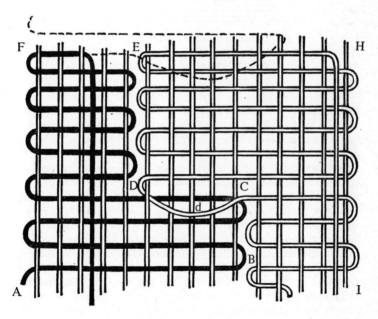

Fig. 10. Diagram showing the formation of seams between two colour sections.
These seams appear at DE and BC.

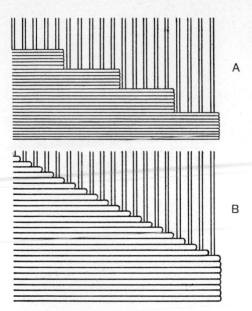

Fig. 11. Connecting two planes of colour along an oblique line is usually achieved by means of steps. A: often used. B: less often used.

When however in bordering sections the change of colour (and therefore of thread) occurs not always at the same two warp threads lying next each other, but is spread continuously over a succession of these threads, the *hachure* is used – one of the most important artistic devices of the technique. We may compare it to the indication of shadow in a drawing by means of hatching. In this case, the term implies the imparting of light and shade by means of narrow stripes, sometimes differing only slightly from each other in colour, so as to create an impression of plastic forms. This effect is achieved by letting the adjacent colours intermingle with each other like flames (fig. 12).

This method was not always in use. The need for it arose as the rendering of plastic forms began to be recognised as the *ne plus ultra* of the art. Before then, in the eleventh, twelfth and thirteenth centuries, the weavers worked in planes of colour simply set beside each other, without transition, as in the wall paintings of the time. Above all, they respected then the essential nature of the plane surface. In the period of decline also, when the weavers merely tried to imitate paintings, hachure was rarely employed.

The flowering of this technique coincided with the increasing number of colours that were put at the weaver's disposal. Obviously, the use of few colours means few transitions can be made between light and shade. As more colours became available, there was an increased possibility of making the transition from light to shade smoother, by means of an ever more refined use of hachures. At last they were able, with these fine hachures, to follow the details of a design exactly, for instance in the folds of a garment (fig. 13).

2. The materials employed

On the topic of colours: in the Middle Ages and even as late as the Renaissance, people knew and used relatively few – namely, blue, red, yellow, green, brown, white, black and ash-grey. There were, certainly, a few shades of each colour at their disposal. It is astounding, nevertheless, with what limited materials the workers of olden days were able to achieve the mastery of colour shown in their works.

By the fourteenth century a total range of 20 to 24 colours and shades was quite common. But already by the sixteenth century the colour range was greatly extended, and in the great

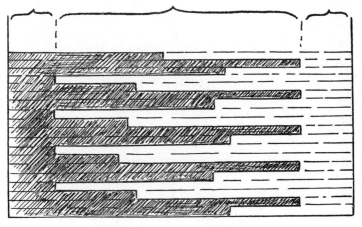

Fig 12. Diagram of a simple hachure.

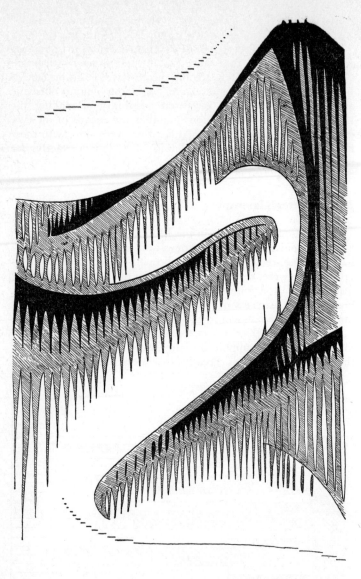

Fig. 13. Application of hachures when indicating, for example, folds in a garment.
Part of a tapestry from Tournai, c. 1460.

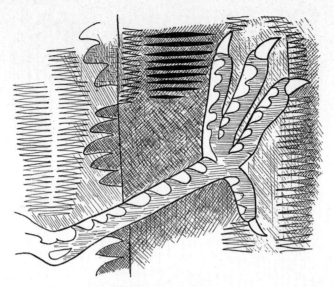

Fig. 14. Hachures in the background give a little variety to the colouring. Part of a tapestry from Delft, 1665.

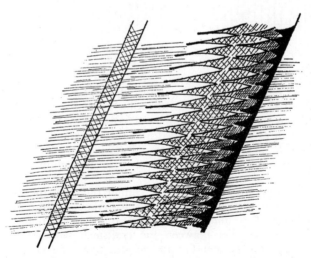

Fig. 15. Method used for indicating light and shade in long, upright objects – for instance a staff or spear.

23

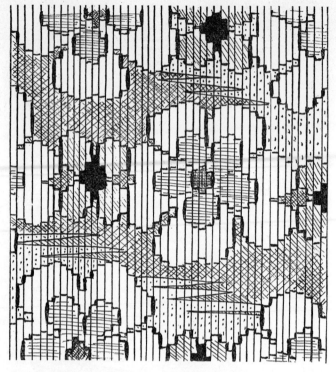

Fig. 16. The impression of shade, by means of splits, used as a 'technique'. Part of a tapestry from Tournai, c. 1460.

ateliers of the eighteenth century the weavers had at their disposal as many as 1500 to 1800 different variegations.

This increase in the number of possible colours, however, cannot in every way be called a change for the better. These tints were used in particular to imitate the art of the painter. Time has shown that the old colours of former centuries endure best.

For this course of events one cannot reproach the master-craftsmen in the great businesses. Not they but the famous painters of their time must be held responsible. There was a well-known conflict between the craftsmen working at the loom, and the painter Oudry, who directed the factories at Beauvais in the first half of the eighteenth century. For their part, the craftsmen accused him of lacking knowledge of their metier, but he managed to impose his will on them: namely, that their highest aim must be to apply in tapestry those conceptions to which he and his contemporaries deferred in the realm of the painter's art.

When Oudry died, at his funeral the head craftsman expressed his opinion that, though the deceased had certainly been a luminary as a painter, he had not shone where tapestry was concerned. Not the painter but the professional has been proved right in the end.

As regards the dyeing of raw materials: usually this was done by one dyer for all the businesses in the town. These dyers, like the owners of ateliers where the tapestry itself was made, were generally highly-esteemed citizens who received many privileges from town governments, such as exemption from military duties and from the payment of rates and tolls.

Wool was the principal material used. In the wefts, linen was employed only occasionally, for example, in the whites of eyes. Of the many sorts of wool available, English and Spanish headed the list; for work of high quality, these were always preferred.

For that matter, whatever the country of origin, in tapestries the best kind of wool was always used – that is to say, wool sheared only from live and healthy sheep, not taken from carcasses.

Once we consult old receipt books, it becomes clear that the methods of preparing wool in different towns was sometimes curious indeed, and that to enhance the quality of the material, nothing was left untried. All kinds of means, some that seem odd to our ears, were for example used in extracting the grease from the wool.

From a note made in 1568, it appears among other things that the writer held the opinion that the Paris ateliers of his day were flourishing because – you would never guess – of compulsory wine-drinking by the staff. These official 'gobelin-drinkers' as they came to be called later on, were supplemented when necessary by soldiers, students, and even by criminals under sentence of death. And the reason for all this? Merely because by this means a certain liquid by-product could be obtained that possessed very special qualities for degreasing the wool. In many receipts, urine formerly played in general a greater role than is now the case.

From the fifteenth century onward, silk comes to the fore in the important centres of France and the Netherlands as a raw material for tapestries. Again, there were great differences in quality amongst the materials on offer. Once more it was Spain that produced the most valuable sorts, especially Granada. This costly silk was used less for ordinary weaving than for sewing up the splits.

From Italy came the expensive organzine silk, which the weavers used by choice only for details in face and hands.

In the same century, the use of gold and silver thread came into favour. Here, a type of gold thread called 'Cyprus thread' was regarded as the best. This costly material became widely used particularly in the fifteenth century. The metal, stuck on a piece of gut, was wound on to a silk thread. Occasionally the gold thread was even introduced into the tapestry with a needle, as in embroidery. Besides the fifteenth century tapestries in the Burgundian collections, those of the time of Louis XVI especially used much gold in the borders.

From a purely artistic viewpoint, fault can be found in the use of metal thread for wall-tapestries. Metal does not absorb light, as wool does, but reflects it. The old weavers, with their well-developed taste, preferred using gold-coloured wool or silk in place of actual gold. Silver thread has the additional objection that in the long run it tarnishes. This also applies to silver-gilt thread, unless the gilding is done with exceptional care.

Naturally, the use of such materials depended on the stipulated price. To us it seems strange that in these transactions the quantity of silk required is measured by weight. The price was also influenced by the number of warp threads per inch on the loom – this number could vary between ten and twenty-five.

Silk was only used for imparting highlights, in flesh for example, in order to emphasise a contrast; never to indicate shadow. Working up light silk in this way perhaps gave rise to the use of the peculiar Dutch word *hoogsel*, found in contracts again and again, and freely used in reference to a portion in light-coloured silk.

We have now come to an aspect of the subject which really calls for more thorough treatment than can be given here. This word *hoogsel* brings up the question of other words that recur time and again in old contracts, about the meaning of which we are not always sure. For example, the word *afsetter*. It may be as well in this connection to say a few words first about the social position of the weavers; the many manipulations their products had to undergo; the great demands made upon them – in short, about their struggle for existence.

3. About the people who made the tapestries

We can say in general that, when the art of tapestry was in full swing, as in the fifteenth, sixteenth and seventeenth centuries, the bigger workshops were in the hands of entrepreneurs who geared the whole industry to the profit motive. Commissions and sales were looked after by dealers whom we can hardly compare to salesmen, since as well as business experience they had to be accustomed to handling money and credit, and might more properly be described as 'merchant tapissers'.

Those in charge of the bigger concerns must have had a great deal of capital at their disposal, for materials were expensive and their outlay was large. The goods were long in the making, and the merchant frequently had a correspondingly long wait for his payment, and furthermore he required large business premises.

Running the workshop was a director with great power over his subordinates. He could for example have slovenly work pulled out, and the weaver concerned received no payment.

It goes without saying that in the various towns the well-nigh all-powerful guildmaster also exercised this right.

Aside from a few outstanding masters of the craft, the weavers themselves were in no very enviable position, as we judge it nowadays. How long in those days used the weavers to work? Their day by our standards was not excessively long, about eight hours on average, though when commissions so required they might continue working until the clock struck ten of an evening. Those in charge must certainly have sought their consent to this overtime, but apparently it was readily given. We know about times and hours of work from jottings made during the fifteenth, sixteenth and seventeenth centuries. They apply to the great centres in what is now Belgium as well as in France.

In rural cottage-industry, where small tapestries, cushions and so forth were made by entire families working together, hours of work would undoubtedly have been longer.

Such working-hours make one ask whether these people were obliged to work by artificial light, and how they managed.

Did that not make for difficulties, working with colours? Would not the source and quality of light have its effect on the choice of colours?

Now our weavers were perfectly aware of this phenomenon, and so of the objections to working by artificial light. The rule in

27

general was in fact that such work should not be done. Though if commissions were many or an important client in a hurry, then ... why, in those days too they knew the difference between what the law lays down, and what is tolerated in practice.

The lighting was extremely primitive. The weaver hung a little wooden box by a hook from the buttonhole of his jacket. In the box stood a burning candle. That was all (figs. 17 and 18).

Danger of fire? That was up to the weaver himself. The nature of his work was such that he usually sat quietly on his bench; in the making of large tapestries, on which he was mostly engaged, he had only to be mindful of working in close teamwork with the mates sitting on either side of him.

The difficulty of colour-changes they anticipated as far as possible by laying out the necessary spools beforehand, in daylight. In this too, the many workmen engaged on the larger tapestries needed good cooperation.

Apart from the apprentices, whose job was to wind the coloured wool on spools, and hand them over or lay them by, the weavers themselves did not all possess the same degree of skill. Their status varied in consequence, as did their part in making the tapestry – and of course, their wage.

Outstanding were the weavers capable of rendering human features just as the draughtsman intended. They were highly regarded and had little to fear from competition. These were men who could ask what they liked, and for whom the workshop rules and penalties did not apply. Weavers who were able to represent the other unclothed parts of the human body also stood high in repute, as did those who could render the sometimes extremely intricate patterns of sixteenth century pomegranate motifs. The lifelike weaving of animals also required

Fig. 17. *Lighting apparatus for the high-warp loom.*

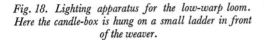

Fig. 18. Lighting apparatus for the low-warp loom. Here the candle-box is hung on a small ladder in front of the weaver.

skills that by no means every weaver possessed. Finally, at the bottom of the ladder, were those who might only help in laying large flat stretches of background, or parts showing sky, where the colour hardly varied.

All however were bound in every possible way to the trade. Frequently the management even controlled their private correspondence, since technical particulars were always considered a local trade secret. And so they must have been, to some extent – witness what was said above as regards the dyeing of wool.

Employers invariably tried to stop the workers leaving their job and moving to another town to look for work. The penalties with which they were threatened if they risked this are to our present ideas unbelievably severe, consisting sometimes in the confiscation of their possessions by the former employer. Such labour relations were not uncommon in former centuries. The history of the textile industry, not to mention other trades, shows many such examples of rigour.

This however was not all. In the nature of the case, the trade employing these men was sensitive to circumstances, and liable therefore to endless fluctuations. Most of all, a gigantic state

29

industry like that in Paris in the seventeenth and eighteenth centuries must have reflected all the ups and downs of the state, particularly of its revenues. There was more than once no money in that enterprise to pay the weavers their due wages, not to mention promised and well-earned bonuses.

Yet those employed in big towns might well be envied by their counterparts in the country, where men did work farmed out by the great ateliers at starvation wages, so as at least to keep bread in their families' mouths.

This state of affairs naturally led to all sorts of malpractices, such as the buying and working up of inferior material, and the delivery of slipshod work.

We have now to mention certain shabby practices in the noble art of tapestry-making, involving among others the *afsetters*. Not that the afsetter – who might, by analogy with photography, be called the retoucher – was the only one who did wrong. When the finished tapestry had been washed and cleaned by the cloth-shearer, the afsetter had the job of touching up the colours and contours with chalk. For this purpose, wet paint must never be used.

Or was it, now and then?

We are almost bound to think it was, for already by the reign of the Emperor Charles V, complaints have arisen about paint being used in tapestries. A regulation of the year 1544, which lays down that in every case the head of a figure must be actually woven, speaks eloquently.

It is certainly the case that retouchers were bound down by many regulations, and strictly controlled. They could skilfully colour whole stretches of the fabric's woollen thread after it had been woven. How far this malpractice prevailed it is difficult now to establish. The famous ateliers seem not to have been guilty of it.

How narrowly use and abuse are divided becomes plain when we read that retouchers had full permission to freshen the colours of tapestries that had become faded. This retouching, however, was in fact officially inspected, so was done according to rule, and, after that, no one was allowed to alter anything in the tapestry.

Anyone at all acquainted with the weaving technique realises that the splits in the tapestry had to be sewn together, and much use was made of this fact. Different ateliers adopted the method of letting portions of a large tapestry be made at the same time on different looms, later piecing the fragments together. The driving need to finish big and profitable orders on time gave rise to this practice.

It was of course possible, by making use of existing detail drawings, to have a tapestry made that presented a completely different composition from the original design which the details had formed.

That original designs were often used in a highhanded way is only to be expected at a time when no copyright was known.

From the fifteenth century onwards, the edges or borders of the tapestries were also woven separately and then sewn on.

After sewing, the complete tapestry was once again given a most thorough inspection, to get rid of what were known as 'lice'. These were portions of warp still visible because the weft threads in those places had not been pushed together firmly enough.

The tapestries were often wholly or partly lined. When the necessary hanging-rings had been sewn on a band of strong material along the upper edge, the tapestry was ready for despatch. This again was looked after by specialists.

These *pacqueurs* were responsible for seeing to the long journeys the tapestries sometimes had to make. Packing had to be done with the greatest care, especially for delivery overseas. Enormous sums of money were at stake. Usually the packers rolled up the tapestries and sewed them in a stout cover that could withstand hard treatment.

4. The border of the tapestry

The development of tapestry borders, edgings or frames deserves a chapter to itself, not only because borders were designed by special draughtsmen, but also because their style followed its own way and made its own rules. This development of course could only begin when tapestries were provided with borders. In the fourteenth and even in part of the fifteenth century, this point had not been reached. When great lords were obliged to travel continually about their domains, consuming on the spot the victuals their land produced, so as to enjoy at least a minimum of comfort, tapestries often formed part of their luggage. Their sombre castles were made more habitable by the hanging of tapestries.

A true border could be contrived only when the tapestries were permanently installed, so that measurements could be adapted accordingly. The measurements depended of course on the wall space, and the amount of clearance around the design itself determined the breadth of the border.

In a few cases, the tapestries conformed to regular measurements, for instance, in those tapestries made specially to fill the gaps between pillars in castle chapels. The gaps in different chapels were generally of the same size, so if needs be the tapestries intended for them could be made in advance.

From about the middle of the fifteenth century more attention was bestowed on the way of enclosing the tapestry. When the design was based on architectural motifs, as in the so-called tabernacle tapestries, the edges of course were indicated by pillars or some other structural theme. These motifs may help to determine the tapestry's date of origin, since renaissance details, obviously, are different from late gothic. Then come the true borders. Leaves, flowers and fruit twine round a sort of hollow frame with a dark base.

In Italy, another sort of border developed – the so-called grotesque, after the well-known ornament of the same name, worked into the borders, which in Raphael's time began its triumphant march across Europe, having been adapted from the decorations in the 'grottoes', recently identified as what remained of Nero's golden mansion.

The borders slowly became ever richer and broader, being divided into lozenges, oblongs and squares, filled in their turn with all sorts of flower and fruit motifs.

During the sixteenth century, every atelier of importance had its own collection of border designs, which, however, were lent and borrowed. It had become the custom now to make centrepiece and border separately. As experts were set to work on different parts of the border, this specialisation was taken even further.

Thus centrepiece and border went each its own way, though it is worth noting that in a given period the border reflects every influence in the general development of style, while the centrepieces continue to repeat the well-established ideas and methods of composition. In view of this development, it is very difficult to assess the wealth of border forms.

Generally speaking, the borders in the sixteenth century became steadily more abundant in detail. Festoons of fruit alternating with armorial scrolls were involved in a whole that might well include trellis work with the addition of bunches of flowers, human figures and so forth. The entire border formed a

32

I. a. The opening of the fourth seal. – "and behold a pale horse, and his name that sat on him was Death, and Hell followed with him." (Rev. 6: 7–8.) b. The worshipping of the dragon, right, and the beast, left, that rose up out of the sea. (Rev. 13: 4–6.) Both tapestries are attributed to the atelier of Nicolas de Bataille. Designed by Hennequin de Bruges. French, late fourteenth century.

II. a. This tapestry, presumably a part, shows on the one hand influences of the distinguished French tapestry-art, and on the other a certain provincialism in technique and execution. The oldest tapestry so far found in Czecho-Slovakia, probably originated in South Germany. End of the fifteenth century. b. and c. Details of a., in which the structure of the weave may be clearly discerned.

tapestry in itself, so much that more than once it rivalled the centrepiece.

In the seventeenth century, new types of enclosure came to the fore. Especially under the influence of Rubens, border and centrepiece again grew into one, because the lower margin was omitted, and the sidepieces were indicated by pillars, which in turn bore a superstructure forming the tapestry's upper margin. The representation thus appeared like a stage-set between the wings.

Lebrun, manufacturing in seventeenth century Paris, maintained more strictly the principle of the border. They were extremely varied, however, filled with flowers and fruit winding around the margin.

The eighteenth century preferred gilded and richly sculpted picture frames, in keeping with the preference for the minute imitation of painting.

The process of development ends as it began: namely, with no border or a very narrow one, as in the time when tapestries were simply stretched over the walls, from the wainscot below to the ceiling above, and from one corner of the room to the other, like a sort of wall paper.

The gilded picture frames mentioned above were also often used for the eighteenth century *verdures* – that is, tapestries largely filled with foliage designs.

II Tapestry to the Beginning of the Middle Ages

Tapestry in Antiquity, in the Early Christian and in the Byzantine period of the Eastern Empire, and among the peoples of Islam, to the beginning of the Middle Ages in the West

If we take 'the history of tapestry' in a strict and literal sense, then this chapter must fail for lack of data. Textile is certainly not the material best suited to endure through the centuries. This as we have seen is particularly true of tapestries hung on walls. Not surprisingly, therefore, the oldest still on view are scarcely ten centuries old.

But it would be a great mistake to conclude from this that the art of making tapestries can only look back on a tradition of a thousand years. The technique described in the chapter on basic principles is incomparably older, to begin with. We ought probably to look on it as one of the most primitive forms of weaving, and as such it has been and still is practised by nearly every people in the world, insofar, at any rate, as they have developed beyond the yet older stage of simple plaiting.

Fig. 19. Greek horseman wearing a cloak plainly showing the characteristics of the fabric. The design appears on a Greek vase of the sixth century B.C.

Traces of this technique are to be found among the most ancient Asiatic nomads as well as the Indians of Peru; among the Ancient Egyptians as well as medieval European peasants.

There is even reason to believe that we ought to have in mind *this* technique, rather than weaving in the literal sense, when Homer tells us of the magnificent garments worn by Hera, or made by Penelope for Odysseus, or kept by Andromache for Hector. Pictures on old Greek vases give us a glimpse of designs that strongly recall those of present-day *kelims*, and no doubt came into being in the same way (fig. 19).

But all this does not alter the fact that few if any tapestries from such ancient times have been preserved – and such tapestries are not necessarily wall-hangings. If we keep an open mind on the subject, and allow that discovered remains may perhaps be fragments of a tapestry, then we may indeed go further back in time.

The oldest tapestry-woven fragments which can be dated with certainty, as they bear the names of Amenhotep II (c. 1449–1423 B.C.) and Thutmosis III (1503–1449 B.C.), were discovered in the tomb of the Egyptian king Thutmosis IV. The largest fragment, with the name of Amenhotep II, has warp threads bent out of parallel, indicating that it was woven on an upright loom, with loomweights to hold the warp taut rather than a beam. The decoration of the fragment consists of a diaper of lotus and papyrus flowers, with the 'uraei', the serpents of Egypt, wearing the crowns of the North and South Kingdoms. It is not unlikely that such carpets served in Egyptian palaces as hangings dividing two rooms, and served that purpose in the funeral decorations. Only the climatic conditions and burial-customs of the land of the Pharaohs could have enabled such a fragment to survive.

This piece is unique, and except for it we must for many centuries be satisfied with written evidence, such as the story of the Jewish girl Esther, who became wife of the Persian emperor Ahasuerus, the Artaxerxes of secular history. Her story is told in the Book of Esther, in the Old Testament. The narrator can scarcely find words to describe the magnificence of the royal dwellings. He speaks of the forecourt of the imperial palace at Shushan: "where were white, green and blue hangings, fastened with cords of fine linen and purple to silver rings and pillars of marble". These hangings may have been tapestries. Of all this splendour, nothing of course remains.

The tapestry fragment next in seniority to the Egyptian ones is a round thousand years younger. It was found at Kerch on the northern shore of the Black Sea. The next pieces that can be dated bring us nearly ten centuries closer to the present time. They too were found in Egypt. They are remains of apparel and tapestries buried with the dead as protective coverings in their last dwellingplace.

Have we any indication of the purpose for which these tapestries were used at the time – that is to say, in the fourth, fifth and sixth centuries after Christ? In the famous mosaics at Ravenna in Italy, depicting the Emperor Justinian and his wife Theodora, tapestries or patterned silk curtains can be seen hanging in front of the passage-ways through which the princely retinue has entered. These mosaics were made in the sixth century. Further evidence is provided by a mosaic in the St. Apollinare Nuovo, also in Ravenna, made somewhat earlier, but still in the sixth century. It represents part of the palace of King Theodoric, and there too, between white marble pillars, hang what could be tapestries (fig. 20).

In all the cases mentioned, we presumably have to do with tapestries made of wool, as remains that have been found suggest. This however began to change when the Byzantines under Justinian became acquainted with the secret of silkworm cultivation.

Legend has it that monks returning from China concealed silkworm eggs inside their hollow walking-sticks, and so were able to bring them across the various frontiers.

From then on, in the princely circles of the capital, silken clothes became the fashion, and undoubtedly silken wall hangings also began to rival those of wool. For all that, the old technique was never wholly superseded by the coming of the new material, as is shown by the existence of silken tapestries made in the manner already described.

Should one now enquire as to the origin of tapestry in its strict sense, it will be found among the peoples of the near and far east, tent-dwellers accustomed to a wandering life. From earliest times, they have covered the desert sands beneath their feet and the tent roof overhead with tapestry-woven carpets. In the thirteenth and fourteenth centuries B.C., the ancient Jewish tribes wandering through the wilderness knew this way of life, and consequently the use of carpets for walls and floors. The movable dwelling of their god Jehovah was completely covered inside with fine linen tapestries, hung from loops, that draped the walls. The dwellings of desert peoples must all satisfy

36

Fig. 20. Tapestry curtains in the sixth century A.D. In nearly all churches of the time, curtains were hung between pillars in the nave, as shown here. (Mosaic in the St. Apollinare Nuovo, Ravenna.)

the same conditions, and be made of light materials and easy to move. The only light furnishings available in the desert were woven materials in the form of tent cloths.

It is surely no accident then that even today when seeking handsome carpets, woven or knotted, for wall or floor, we procure them chiefly from central-Asiatic and eastern peoples who still for the great part live in an extremely primitive way.

In these regions the *kelim* is still made. Here the ancient technique of tapestry-weaving has been practised throughout the centuries, although knotted-pile carpets have gained more ground.

It was the Arabs who, in their march on the west during the seventh century, not only preserved this art where they found it, but were able to stimulate a new florescence, witness the discoveries in Egypt and Spain.

III Tapestry in the Middle Ages

Tapestry in the Middle Ages, particularly in the four-teenth century (Arras) and the fifteenth century (Arras and Tournai)

As we are now going to concern ourselves in particular with the evolution of tapestry in Western Europe, we must bear in mind that the flowering of this art in the countries we have now to consider was based on the previous development in the east. After being cultivated there for many centuries, tapestry-weaving was to flourish anew here in the west, achieving a perfection unknown hitherto in the east. How and exactly when this fertilising influence occurred is not now entirely clear, but of the fact itself, however, there is no doubt. That the more highly-developed east in the centuries following the Crusades was the donor in this realm of art, and the west the recipient, is clear from, for instance, the old appelation 'tapissier Sarrasinois' (Saracen tapisser) which was constantly used in the thirteenth century when referring to a certain type of weaver, as well as from indications that people even in the fifteenth century referred to the tapestries themselves as 'paynim work'.

No doubt the technique was already known here, along with the material, but the arrival in the Eastern Empire of the silkworm and thus of silken fabrics excited new possibilities, even for those with no access yet to the new thread. They could at least try using the familiar materials in the old manner to imitate the magnificent Byzantine silks.

Thus the oldest piece of tapestry we possess, made for certain in the west, is an imitation of a Byzantine silk fabric. Different museums have each a portion of this tapestry. It was made about the year 1000, somewhere on the German Rhine. It is a pity that no more have survived, since written sources and particularly wall paintings and miniatures from this and earlier centuries give us adequate information about the use of these tapestries.

In the paintings, the 'tapetum' or 'tapetis', including the rings from which it used to hang, can be seen on the lower courses of church walls, and behind the backrests of the choir stalls. In the miniatures, we see them hanging over the backs of princely thrones. These cloths continually display Byzantine motifs, but of the technique and materials we know nothing, and so can draw no conclusions for our theme.

Clearly in these times, from the ninth up to and including the thirteenth century, we must expect to find our tapestries chiefly in churches and palaces.

Churches are mentioned before palaces, by intention. Places of worship were then being built everywhere, however small, and we may look on them as probably the oldest sales outlet; while in the monasteries, closely connected with them, we find the oldest centres of production.

Some of the oldest tapestries are still preserved in convents. These are back cloths, which used to hang, as already mentioned, behind and above the backs of the choir stalls, like those placed against the walls of the church.

They are about ten yards long and a yard in width, and are to be found in the small town of Halberstadt in Germany. Both tapestries – for there are two of them – were made in the twelfth century: the Angel tapestry, so-called, in about 1130, and the so-called Apostle tapestry half a century later. The first of them shows, successively: the angels visiting Abraham (Gen 18:2), the sacrifice of Isaac (Gen. 22:1–19) and the Archangel Michael fighting the dragon (Rev. 12:7). A fourth part representing Jacob's dream (Gen. 28:10–15) has been lost.

The Apostle tapestry shows us Christ enthroned on a rainbow, with Michael and Gabriel to his left and right. Next to these stand six apostles on either side. A part of this tapestry representing Christ among the four Evangelists has also been lost.

In both tapestries, the Byzantine influence is very great. The figures in each have the stiff faces with dark-rimmed, almond-shaped eyes that are characteristic also of the paintings of the period. They were in all probability made in a convent in the close neighbourhood, for example in Quedlinburg.

In Halberstadt yet another detail of a wall carpet is to be found; this, however, dates from the beginning of the thirteenth century. It depicts within a lozenge shape the Emperor Charlemagne, with four philosophers around him. All the pieces made in Germany about this time are relatively small, probably because the size of the looms would not allow the making of larger areas.

As it happens, the art of embroidery was flourishing throughout these centuries. Once it was past its zenith, tapestry had a better chance to thrive.

Germany, which during the centuries that followed had no court life at the centre, on which the whole commonwealth could focus, had however little or no part in this. We shall return to Germany in a separate chapter.

Centres prominent in the development of tapestry must be looked for in those lands where kings had been able to build up a centrally-directed sovereign authority, such as France in the fourteenth century. Almost nothing, curiously enough, has been preserved from the centuries before. Then slowly comes increasing evidence to give us some insight into the nature of the tapestries that were used.

For this information we are chiefly indebted to descriptions that occur in romances of chivalry – the current form of literary art in those days – when referring to the vivid painting of a castle interior. Judging by these descriptions, the tapestries hung against the walls there showed scenes from the scriptures and mythology, and heroic deeds of ancestors whose memory was still alive.

Expressly mentioned are the exploits of Charlemagne and his paladins, among whom was always shown in a place of distinction Guillaume d'Orange, better known as Guillaume le Cornet, – the horn that princes of the House of Orange still bear in their coat of arms.

It cannot, alas, be known for certain whether the tapestries there mentioned were all tapestries in the sense ascribed to them in this book.

In the twelfth and thirteenth and even during the fourteenth century, there is every reason to take into account as wall-hangings embroidered cloths as well as woven stuffs, both then used as we use wall paper, to cover the walls around us. The Bayeux tapestry (which is not tapestry-woven) is a fine example of an early embroidered hanging, while woven hangings are shown in the miniature by Fouquet, 'Lit de Justice', the action against the Duc d'Alençon, in 1458, presided over by King Charles VII.

Although we possess so few tangible remains of this period, it was precisely then that the conditions came into existence which made possible the enormous development of tapestry-making as a large-scale industry.

About this time, it happened that the castles of the high nobility were notably modernised and enlarged. The donjon or keep, usually a round tower, extremely simple and heavily-fortified, was in the fourteenth century more and more frequently abandoned, or at least enlarged with big rectangular rooms, more pleasant for living in.

Thus arose not only the possibility but also the necessity of giving these large wall-spaces now available a warm covering, at any rate during the time of residence. The custom, current in southern lands, of covering such walls with frescoes, had certainly also been put into practice in the North, though not to the same extent as, for example, in Italy. The climate was less favourable to this form of art, and the inhabitants required more shelter. The tapestry was practical, and satisfied the needs of personal comfort.

A tapestry would be hung by iron rings from heavy rods, so that a narrow passage would always be left between the tapestry and the wall. The servants commonly found their way along these narrow thoroughfares.

The wind would set these monstrous hangings lightly stirring, so that, especially of an evening or at night, when dim candle-flame or mere moonlight rendered the figures scarcely visible, all sorts of ghost stories were born. On dark nights the figures in the tapestry would vanish away by mysterious means, only to take their places again next morning, in ways equally difficult to explain.

So far as the number of tapestries then used is concerned, our chief source of knowledge for those centuries is the inventory lists of the French kings. We can be fairly sure from these that the reigning monarchs and their kinsmen must by the fourteenth century have had at their disposal considerable numbers of tapestries.

To find out something more of the manner in which the tapestrymakers conceived their work, we must take into account the related branches of pictorial art of which we happen to know more – namely, miniatures on the one hand and wall paintings on the other. Let us begin by pointing out that both these branches of art, like tapestry itself, must be thought of in close connection with the written word. The same subject-matter that was noted down by the 'clerks' from the mouths of singers, is also to be found treated of in wall paintings, just as in tapestries and miniatures. Bearing in mind the exclusive and self-contained milieu for which they painted, sang and made their tapestries, this should be self-evident.

When the courtly adventure-romances, for example, supplanted the rhymed chronicles, and the writer of these romances identified the character of the reigning prince – on whose benevolence he was wholly dependent – with the hero he described with such verve, and did not even hesitate to compare his prince with one of the heroes of antiquity – then the tapestry too would soon reproduce the same theme. Again, the intention would be to do homage to the prince, presented in the person of the hero. Hence there is early mention of tapestries which depict Alexander the Great, Aeneas, Hercules and Caesar.

Under Philip the Good a new source of inspiring themes was exploited – a source with which all those able to follow the literature of their times were already more or less familiar.

These were the stories that had long been current, from the Celtic world in the west, on the one hand, and on the other, those brought by the Crusaders from the east. By then, the period of the Crusades lay far enough in the past to make the stuff of epics.

Beside the religious subjects that continued to retain their place in the tapestries, there now appeared as if by magic such figures as King Arthur and the Knights of the Round Table, the story of the Holy Grail, Lancelot, Parsifal and Lohengrin, Tristan and Iseult, Jason and the Golden Fleece.

Decisions as to this choice of material were of course not made without taking into account the opinion of the person ordering the tapestry. The Burgundian aristocracy, and particularly Charles the Bold, were extremely fond of reading these romances.

The mystery plays, so-called – religious dramas first performed in church, and later in the open air – and the pantomimes, as they were styled – staged at the courts of princes – are other expressions of medieval culture which also exercised great influence on the subjects people liked to find depicted in tapestry.

The mystery plays were principally concerned with religious themes, giving representations for example of the finding of the True Cross by the Empress Helena, mother of Constantine; the resurrection of Christ; the battle between the Archangel Michael and the Devil; the Last Supper, and so forth.

In the pantomimes, scenes were performed showing Orpheus amid the animals, the story of Perseus and Andromeda, the education of Achilles, Hercules defeating the centaurs, and the usual mythological subjects.

We can rediscover a major part of these performances on the tapestries. The hero-worship, too, is still appropriate in a time when the moods of Christianity and antiquity are mingled together. Thus tapestries were made depicting the principal heroes of the Jews, the pagans and the Christians, in groups of three. They were, respectively: Joshua, David and Judas Maccabeus; Hector, Alexander and Caesar; and King Arthur, Charlemagne and Geoffrey of Bouillon as the three highly venerated 'worthies' of Christendom. And it will come as a surprise to no one that tapestries featuring heroines soon made their appearance also.

As already mentioned, religious themes maintained their position of importance, but the great lords now began to show a certain preference for figures out of history or Holy Writ who might be supposed to have some close connection with their own rank in life, or to serve as active exemplars. Thus St George and St Theodorus appeared in tapestries, David the victor over Goliath of Gath, and Jephtha who slew the Midianites, Gideon and his chosen men, Samson the strong, and so on.

As for the New Testament as a source of themes, there is scarcely one happening that did not come to be represented. They even pursued the subject still further, reaching back to those legendary figures, the sibyls, who were supposed to have foretold Christ's birth. In painting we see the same thing happening. We have but to bear in mind the famous painting by Michelangelo on the ceiling of the Sistine chapel.

Together with subjects such as these, with which people eagerly surrounded themselves so as to display their reading, erudition and good taste, a theme was slowly coming to the fore which bore a real and direct relation to the courtly and knightly life of the upper classes – namely, the chivalrous conception of love.

This will indeed be self-evident to those who know something of the remarkable contrasts, even contradictions, in the relations between the sexes in the knightly culture of the twelfth and thirteenth centuries. Man's service to woman furnished themes for centuries, not only for tapestries, but also for paintings and book-illumination.

Intricately concealed, yet often clearly to be perceived in the guise of hunting-scenes, games, tourneys and gatherings of companions in garden and bower, this 'love-service' under its many allegories and symbols, full of riddles and double-entendre, found a place in tapestries. The same development can be observed in the embroidering of clothes. Here too appeared a superabundance of riddles, symbols and allegories.

Only towards the end of the fourteenth century, in the time of the Black Death, when the plague moved across Europe, did this game of love give ground to abominable brutality, not least in the mutual relation of man and woman. The theme had however not been rejected for good, for presently it returned, this time in the significant form of the so-called *Wildeman* (variously known as a Woodwol, Woodwose or Woodhouse – a wild man) or rustic tapestries, which show the reaction of the over-refined courtier to his cultivated life, and by idealising the state of nature thus give a foretaste of what awaits us in eighteenth-century France.

According to other interpreters, however, the representations on these (allegorical) tapestries relate much more to the strife between good and evil. In this sphere also belong the tapestries representing virtues and vices.

To find armorial motifs in a society where the coat of arms played such an important role is not surprising. These tapestries too passed through a development, like those of the group designated by the term 'verdure'. Armorial tapestries and these 'green tapestries' in point of fact have a common origin, in the sense that armorial blazonry was to begin with depicted on a background preponderantly green, usually of leaves.

By a 'verdure' then is to be understood a tapestry on which only leaf motifs are to be found instead of, for example, human figures. They seem to have been made as early as the thirteenth century, and were used particularly in guest rooms and bedrooms. From these simple green tapestries slowly evolved scenes centring around a blossoming tree, which in their turn developed into the portrayal of entire gardens. Placing in the centre a jetting fountain had a spiritual significance to the eye of the initiate – namely Mary, the mother of Our Lord, the source of all life. Verdures were usually not large.

In thinking of tapestries, one is too much inclined to consider only very large examples. This is a misconception. Along with the huge tapestries that now hang for the most part in museums, many small ones were made. Usually the client did not order a single piece, but a set of room-hangings. Such furnishings would generally consist of the tapestries needed to cover the walls and drape the enormously large bed, for which one cloth served as a ceiling, others for the sides and the foot, another to enclose the head of the bed, and finally yet another tapestry to act as bed cover. Included in such a set of furnishings would be other smaller pieces to spread along benches or to put at the disposal of the family's honoured guests.

Summing up in a few words, we can say therefore that in the Middle Ages, tapestry was employed principally in churches, and thereafter in castles where the high nobility resided, in a world cut off from other social classes, where courtly forms and manners disguised autocratic dominion and ambition for power.

Now where were these tapestries made?

Basing themselves on the fact that one single name is known of a 'merchant tapisser' at Paris, famous in his day, people have far too easily assumed that by the fourteenth century an important tapestry industry had been established in the French capital.

Not much fourteenth century work has been preserved, but one series of magnificent tapestries dating from the latter part of the century can still be seen and admired today, in a specially built museum attached to the great castle at Angers in central France. This is the famous series with scenes from the Revelation of St. John, called the Apocalypse, a work of great beauty. From surviving accounts we know that it was commissioned by Louis, Duc d'Anjou from Nicolas Bataille, 'tapissier de Paris', and that it was made for him in the years 1376–1381. Originally the tapestries were nearly twenty feet high and 110 yards long, comprising ninety-six individual panels. Today there are still sixty-nine panels left, totalling more than 100 yards in length, and nearly five yards in height.

The horizontal panels are alternated by vertical ones, in which a tall figure appears over and over again, by a lectern in a richly adorned portico. An open book lies before him (fig. 21). This figure probably represents the visionary of Patmos. The background of the horizontal panels, which show scenes from the Revelation, is blue and red alternately. Only twelve to fifteen colours were used in the entire work.

The designs for this monumental work were made full size by the court painter Jean de Bruges, and based partly on a richly-illuminated manuscript lent for the purpose by the King of France. It seems possible that Nicolas Bataille might have had the tapestries made by his staff actually at his client's castle; but if this were so, the workmen were still from Paris, or possibly from Arras.

The evidence goes to show, that the place where most tapestries of the period were made was not Paris, but Arras in the county of Artois in northern France. The first mention of the place in this connection is only in 1313, it is true, but the tapestry industry must have been established there long before, considering the dimensions and quality of the tapestries then made there.

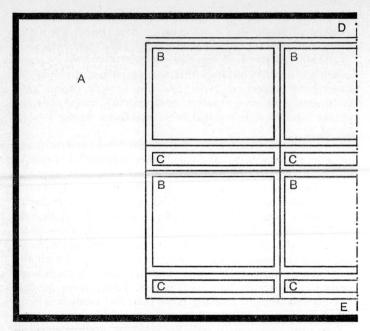

Fig. 21. Diagram reconstructing the original positions of the Apocalypse tapestries, from the portions still in existence. (After Louis de Farcy in Les Tapisseries d'Angers, *René Planchenault.)*

A. *The place on the original tapestries where St. John the Divine was portrayed within a high-arched loggia writing his book.*

B. *Here was the original place of the scenes from the Revelation.*

C. *According to Farcy, this was the position of the texts relating to the scenes above.*

D. *Here was a strip with a sky-scene, with clouds and birds.*

E. *Here was a strip depicting the earth, with flowers, etc.*

The town was already well-known in previous centuries for its flourishing dye-works, to which was added later a highly-developed textile industry. No wonder that here as in so many other Flemish towns came the first great confrontations between the powerful merchants who handled the business and the 'men with the blue fingernails' – the dyers, allied with the weavers. It was here that for the first time a situation developed compelling workers at the loom to choose between the freedom of being their own masters, and taking up employment in the big concerns. Independence meant home industry, making small tapestries and cushions on small looms, working long hours for a wretchedly low rate of pay.

Many worked in this manner, for instance in Lille and Valenciennes. Wage-labour however meant selling oneself, becoming dependent on large-scale industry with its restrictions and lack of liberty.

In Arras and Tournai big business won in the struggle against the free craftsmen. Tapestries that measured five yards high and sometimes thirty yards wide were made here on gigantic looms.

When in 1363 Philip the Bold of Burgundy founded the house that is named after him, this branch of the French royal house began to order tapestries in Arras. The town's products thus achieved European renown, so that in Italy the word 'arazzo' became synonymous with tapestry.

Of all this splendour, alas, scarcely anything remains, or it would perhaps be more accurate to say that identifying these Arras tapestries is extremely difficult. As we have seen, there were many other places in the County of Flanders where the cloth industry had provided work for many hands and put bread in many mouths, which now must look for other means of subsistence. Among these towns was Tournai, which like Arras had for centuries been famous for the products of its looms. Arras alone could not possibly have filled the orders that now came in constantly increasing numbers.

In the fifteenth century the rich Burgundian court displayed ever more pomp and splendour, and what more appropriate expression than an array of luxurious tapestries? They were hung up everywhere the nobility put in an appearance. Particularly on the days when the Chapter of the Order of the Golden Fleece – founded in 1429 – held its assembly, the display of wealth and power was simply overwhelming. Wherever this Chapter chose to assemble, the walls were hung for choice with a famous series of tapestries made in Tournai, depicting scenes from the life of Gideon.

In this town, the best-known merchant tapisser was Pasquier Grenier. From his workshops – he may have owned ateliers in Brussels and Arras as well – came a stream of most beautiful tapestries.

The Burgundian princes eventually had such a stock of tapestries that under Philip the Good a big stone warehouse was built, and special officers appointed as 'Gardes de la Tapisserie', to keep them in good order.

As well as large tapestries, eleven yards by five, smaller pieces were also made here, like the bedspreads, cushions, tablecloths etc. already mentioned.

Prices were stupendously high, particularly when much gold thread was worked into the tapestry. When a series of any considerable size was paid for, thousands of gold pieces changed hands.

This development was sustained by the flourishing progress of Flemish painting. Tapestries as late as the reign of Charles the Bold (1467–1477) show densely crowded pictures, in which different scenes appear not in succession but actually side by side. Of a sense of space composition there was as yet no indication, and to the designers the patterns on the clothes worn seem to have been more important than the personalities of the wearers. Not until later did the Italian influence have its effect.

A beautiful series showing the Passion of Christ, rendered on four tapestries, may be mentioned as an impressive example of Flemish tapestry from the end of the fifteenth or possibly the beginning of the sixteenth century. As a great French connoisseur of tapestries has observed: "These reflect the emotion and sensibility of the Middle Ages as they approached modern times. The devotion of those times to the Passion is vividly revealed – a devotion vigorously stimulated by the moving sermons of that age, and by the pervasive acting of the mystery plays".

This series, like the Apocalypse tapestries mentioned earlier, is preserved in the chapel of the same castle in Angers.

The capture of Arras by Louis XI in 1477 signified a real calamity for this town. The lead passed entirely, first to Tournai, later to Brussels. For two centuries the latter dominated the entire tapestry industry, for the industry continued despite dynastic changes.

Princes of the house of Austria, who took possession of Flanders after the death of Charles the Bold, also laid up an enormous store of tapestries. The Emperor Maximilian I owned depositories not only in the Netherlands, but also at Innsbruck and Augsburg.

The sixteenth century was to witness an efflorescence of the art in no way inferior to the fifteenth.

III. a. Tapestry from a series on the life of St. Stephen. Probably made at the end of the fifteenth century. The scene shows the choosing of the first deacons by the apostles (Acts 6: 5–6.) In the foreground to the right are Stephen, Philip and Prochorus, and behind them, Nicanor, Timon, Parmenas and Nicolas. The rays of light (top, right) represent the Holy Ghost. b. Tapestry depicting the vintage. This tapestry cannot be dated earlier than the beginning of the sixteenth century.

IV. Both details form part of a series of seven tapestries portraying the life of Jesus, made in a Brussels atelier in the third quarter of the sixteenth century. a. Detail from the tapestry showing Christ washing the disciples' feet. b. Detail from the tapestry showing the deposition from the Cross.

IV Tapestry in the Sixteenth Century

1. Brussels and other centres in the Spanish Netherlands

The war between Louis XI of France and Charles the Bold of Burgundy lasted ten years – a war that inflicted heavy damage on tapestry-weaving in the frontier region between France and Burgundy. Arras had been eliminated, and Tournai passed into French hands. The latter town, deprived of the patronage of Charles, was soon to decline in importance.

Luckily for those inhabiting the Low Country provinces of the kingdom of Burgundy, the new rulers of the house of Austria clearly saw the importance of a flourishing tapestry industry, in which, however, their capital, Brussels, was now to take the lead.

Many artisans, including weavers, had left their homes under stress of war, making their way to places where they hoped to build up a new life in better circumstances.

Naturally enough, it was Brussels that attracted and received most of them. Tapestries had in fact been made in this town in the fifteenth century. The town also possessed good, old-established dye-works. English wool, the best procurable in those days, was delivered through Antwerp in sufficient quantity to enable large orders to be accepted. Big business therefore saw its opportunity, and managed to incorporate many smaller master craftsmen.

This emigration of skilled labour from the south also reached other smaller centres, where the industry had hitherto been practised, but only on a very modest scale. Thus, next to Brussels, Antwerp came to the fore. The merchants in this important port even established an Exchange to handle their products.

Another centre worth mentioning is Oudenaarde, a place supported by its neighbouring villages, where home-workers could take in a part of the commissions.

In the sixteenth century, particularly during the first half, Brussels tapestries reached a new high point of development.

As we have already mentioned briefly, the progress of tapestry is inseparably linked with that of painting. Painting leads the way, tapestry follows. Hugo van der Goes and his school, in the last years of the fifteenth century, had already exercised great influence on the style of tapestry. However, here in the north of Europe, Gothic subject matter and Gothic forms continued to find a place in tapestries, even when elsewhere the Renaissance had already long found favour.

This was due not only to geographical factors, but much more to the resistance by those in power to new ideas, unless they happened to be launched by those in their own circle.

The miniatures show with what devotion the representatives of the intellectual élite dedicated their creations to their paymasters, and, seeing these kneeling figures, we realise that influence on their work was still too much dependent on their subordinate positions.

This conservatism was of course accentuated by the time-consuming way the tapestries were made. A series would sometimes be in hand ten years. And in reading the correspondence between clients and suppliers, it again amazes us how much patience the client had to exercise before seeing the series at last delivered, and – this may well equal matters out – how much patience the suppliers, in their turn, needed before the sums agreed on were paid in full.

Nevertheless, one aspect of the Renaissance quickly received expression, in the art of tapestry as elsewhere, and this aspect was characteristic of the milieu: namely, the glorification of personages and families. In the sixteenth century were commissioned whole sequences of tapestries portraying real or fancied ancestors. (Did not the Burgundian dukes boast of Hercules as the founder of their house?)

At this time too, triumphal processions began to be shown in tapestry, analogous to the progresses and triumphal entries into their cities that princes felt bound to make from time to time, and in which every artist of note had to cooperate.

The personage celebrating the triumph was of course too much of a gentleman to wish to be charged with even a semblance of selfglorification. He therefore never put in an appearance in the triumphal car, but the tapestry-designer took good care that his deeds would be indirectly extolled by introducing an overwhelming quantity of emblems. The car itself was drawn by allegorical animal figures. The idea of a triumphal car in tapestry became so popular that even the church made use of it. There appear, for example, tapestries showing the triumph of Christ.

In many of these tapestries, however, the medieval spirit

continued to be very eloquent. Among these in particular was a certain Master Philip whose impress – that of an artist of genius – was stamped on the tapestries of his time. We may perhaps identify this Master Philip with the painter Philip van Orley, a brother of the better-known painter Bernard van Orley. Master Philip made the designs for more than a hundred tapestries. The great conflict between the conservative Gothic trend, in the north, and that of the Renaissance in the south, beyond the Alps, broke out when the famous 'Acts of the Apostles', after designs by Raphael, were made in Brussels, and became known to everyone involved in the profession.

Next to Master Philip and in cooperation with him, another famous designer worked in Brussels – Jan van Roome, court painter to Margaret of Parma, Regent of the Netherlands.

In a realm that for him was wholly new, Raphael sought to apply to tapestry design contemporary concepts of painting. Bernard van Orley, however, while influenced by the Italian style, maintained the decorative Gothic trend, with its overwhelming richness of detail, particularly in the apparel of the persons portrayed. For that matter, even in Italy not everyone was taken with the result of Raphael's work. His older rival Michelangelo appears not to have greatly appreciated it. The main set of the Acts of the Apostles is now preserved in the Vatican, while seven of Raphael's designs for it are in London, at the Victoria and Albert Museum.

The Flemish master's preference for detail, as it happens, was not only prompted by stylistic considerations, but also prescribed by the technique, in which large, unsubdivided areas do much less to demonstrate the richness of the material than a multiplicity of strongly-detailed forms. Even when Van Orley borrowed his subject-matter from Petrarch he continued in his interpretation of forms to resist the influence from across the Alps.

But evolution was not to be arrested in Brussels, even though it was not until after 1530 that the principles of the High Renaissance, represented by Raphael, broke through the Brussels traditions for good. At first in the background and scarcely visible, later plainer and bigger, Roman ruins slowly but surely appear on the tapestries in the midst of Flemish villages.

In that respect too, painting led the way. The battle was quickly over. Motifs from antiquity, first introduced on the sly in order to extol reigning princes, are now brought to life again for their own sake.

51

Scarcely any classical writer can be named who has not furnished subject-matter for a series of tapestries.

Thus, together with themes already current, we now see the Fall of Icarus, the Abduction of Ganymede, the Punishment of Marsyas and the Rescue of Andromeda making their appearance in tapestries. Though the subject-matter might be old, the way of presenting it was not. This corresponds closely with what is nowadays often expected on the stage – namely, giving the star of the play the dominating position, right before the footlights, or, as we express this on a tapestry, in the foreground. Fellow-actors are little more than supernumeraries, and play a very modest role well in the background of the tapestry.

So great was the renown of Brussels as a manufacturing and trading centre for tapestries of the highest quality that great lords, both temporal and spiritual, with a taste for art, vied with each other in placing orders with the important Brussels manufacturers.

First among these we must mention Pieter van Aelst, not only a man who had numerous businesses under him in Brussels and elsewhere, but also a connoiseur of the subject with whom few could be compared.

He it was who in 1515 received from Pope Leo X the order for manufacturing the series of tapestries, mentioned above, that Raphael designed. In these eleven tapestries, together measuring forty-two yards long and five yards high, only the most skilful weavers were allowed to cooperate.

The work demanded three years of strenuous labour, and the series became so much admired that Van Aelst had to copy it at least four or five times for other clients.

The risks involved, even in – or should we say, particularly in – such large-scale industrial enterprises as these, become very plain when we learn that Van Aelst in his later years fell into great financial difficulties and had to ask for help from such rich money-lenders as, for example, the Fuggers of Augsburg.

His leading place as a merchant was taken over by Pieter de Pannemaker and other members of the Pannemaker family. Like Van Aelst, this man was purveyor to the court, and consequently found himself supplying pretty well all the princely courts of Europe. One of the Pannemakers made the famous series for the Emperor Charles V, depicting among other things the latter's expedition to Tunis in 1535. The designer, Jan Cornelisz Vermeyen, had by royal command to accompany the expedition himself, and portray everything true to life. This sequence of tapestries, twelve in all, had to be undertaken all at the same time, with seven workers at each loom.

Next to their predilection for dramatic classical themes, the princes saw in the rich wall-coverings of their state apartments a chance to record their own great deeds for posterity. The series just mentioned is perhaps the finest example of this kind.

At this time, tapestries on religious subjects were still, however, constantly in demand. The stories of the Passion, the Apocalypse and the Last Judgment, in particular, must have kept the looms busy many times. But these subjects too were treated in a different manner than formerly.

Other ideas had come to the attention of the upper classes, and been eagerly taken up.

Much interest was taken in the *Biblia-pauperum* – the Bible of the Poor – which had been in existence for centuries. People now chose to take these primitive woodcuts, that grouped together and combined similar ideas taken from the Old and New Testaments, according to distinct categories, and use them as inspiration for the extremely refined art of tapestry.

This mention of religion introduces the question whether these luxury industries felt no repercussions of the religious wars which just at this time were tearing Europe apart.

The answer must be – yes, to be sure.

Many tapestry-workers, master craftsmen as well as journeymen and apprentices, fearing persecution as Protestants, emigrated to the north. This of course had its consequences in working-standards as well as subject-matter. In the last decades of the sixteenth century Brussels tapestries therefore show a marked decline in form. The traditional forms were continually imitated, but the attitudes became more bombastic and lost effect. It was for that matter the period of mannerism. Italian influence still continued to be great, and 'grotesque'-tapestries were extremely popular. 'Verdures' were of course also made in Brussels, though this was a share of the market that fell especially to the smaller centres.

2. The region along the Loire

After considering Brussels, we ought not wholly to lose sight of France. After the destruction of Arras, and when Tournai had lost its importance, the tapestry industry revived once more in France – not, however, in the north, but south of Paris in the basin of the Loire, in the part of the country known as Touraine. In this magnificent countryside, in the reigns of Louis XI, who resided at Tours, Charles XIII at Amboise and Louis XII at Blois, the tapestry industry flowered anew. Many ecclesiastical tapestries were made in Tours, characteristically divided by light architectural elements which slowly began to display Renaissance forms in place of Gothic. They are known as tapestries 'en forme de tabernacle', and can be traced as late as the middle of the century. There are fine specimens in the cathedral at Rheims.

The famous 'millefleur' tapestries comprise a much more extensive group, the characteristic background of which is a closely covered field of flowers, frequently on dark blue. The blossoms are simply set beside each other, without overlapping. This sort of tapestry had already come to the fore in the last decade of the fifteenth century, and was being made until about the middle of the sixteenth.

Themes were mainly drawn from the life of knights and courtiers of the time. Chiefly deserving of mention in this splendid group is the set called 'The Lady with the Unicorn', made to the order of Jean de Chabannes, Lord of Vendernesse as a gift for his betrothed, Claude le Viste. At the present day they are in the Cluny Museum in Paris. These six tapestries bring to mind the flowering meadows that in spring adorn the banks of the Loire. Each tapestry has a background of a singularly beautiful red. In each one there stands on a blue-green island, a female figure, sumptuously dressed, with her maid of honour. The most conspicuous among the animals appearing on the tapestry is the unicorn, a symbol in those days of the Immaculate Conception.

The tapestries represent an allegory of the five senses; only the sixth tapestry, showing a pavilion on which appears the superscription 'Mon seul desir' remains enigmatic.

Another remarkable tapestry from this group, also probably made in Tours, shows the Passion of Christ through the medium of the Instruments of the Passion, which are borne by angels. Between the angels a parchment is seen, unrolled, on which events of the Passion are celebrated in octosyllabic verse.

In regions nearby, such as Felletin and Aubusson, tapestries were also being made at the time. In general, they are somewhat less fine in execution, but the style is in keeping with that already mentioned. In these centres tapestries seem particularly to have been made in which flowers and small animals appear.

Of course, cushions were made on the small looms, and here

too they continued to follow the same themes as in the large tapestries. In both cases, this eventually gave rise to a formalistic rigidity.

In the nature of the case, masterpieces such as have been named above are not for sale. These cushions and similar small pieces, however, still make desirable purchases nowadays for those who care for them.

V Tapestry in the Seventeenth Century

1. Paris and other centres in France

We have already briefly indicated that the position the French capital occupied in the fourteenth century with regard to tapestry-weaving is far from clear. The fact that, among others, a famous merchant tapisser like Nicolas Bataille had lived there, receiving orders and fulfulling them, naturally implies at least that these commissions were carried out in Paris by weavers who lived and worked there. Very probably ateliers had already been established in the French capital by that time, but for the present it still remains an open question whether and to what extent the appellation 'tapisserie française' may be identified with Paris as the manufacturing centre. There is no doubt as to the position of Paris in later days, however. About this we are well informed.

As early as the sixteenth century, about the year 1540, King Francis I had set up a tapestry workshop at his castle in Fontainebleau with the help of Flemish weavers. His successor Henry II went a step further, by attaching a tapestry workshop to the Paris orphanage, the 'Hôpital de la Trinité', having made Paris the court capital again. By this means he at any rate managed to solve for the time being the eternal problem of how to come by cheap labour.

Both workshops produced some well-known sets of tapestries, but they only flourished for a short time. Fontainebleau was already becoming unimportant as a purveyor of tapestries by about the middle of the sixteenth century, and although the workshop connected with the orphanage continued to exist into the middle of the seventeenth, it was not with this but with another that the history of the famous name of 'Gobelin' was to be linked.

This story goes back to Henry IV of the house of Bourbon, who in 1607 gave letters patent for the founding of a tapestry workshop in Paris to two Flemings – Marc de Comans and his brother-in-law François de la Planche, properly Van der Planken. This new business, that can safely be regarded as a competitor of the thriving weaving-mills in Brussels and Oudenaarde, achieved a high reputation in seventeenth century France.

Henry IV was extremely tolerant concerning the religion of his subjects, an attitude uncommon at that time. He it was who proclaimed in 1598 the Edict of Nantes, that secured religious freedom for the Huguenots. By granting the non-Catholic weavers freedom to practise the 'reformed religion', he lured back to their own land many who had emigrated north for the sake of their faith.

Thus there was soon neither lack of labour nor of commissions, so that the directors of the business had to look out for other, preferably adjacent premises, because the out-buildings of the Tournelles palace, where they had their looms, proved to be too small.

They obtained the workshops in the Faubourg Saint-Marcel that since 1440 had belonged to the Gobelin family – cloth-dyers of repute, who had done very nicely and raised no objection to disposing of their property for a good price. These premises lay on the bank of a little river, the Bièvre, since the Gobelins' trade could not be practised without running water in the immediate neighbourhood.

It was this name *Gobelin* that later was to become synonymous with tapestry.

Nevertheless, this first 'Gobelin-manufactory', as the workshops of the two Flemings were later called, had to contend with difficulties when the son of Van der Planken walked out of the business and opened an independent workshop in the Faubourg Saint-Germain.

In 1662 came the great change that was to make Paris the centre of the tapestry industry next in importance to Brussels. In that year not only the workshops, but also the dwelling-house of the Gobelins were bought by Louis XIV's great minister, Colbert – he of the mercantile system – naturally on behalf of his young sovereign. Colbert saw very clearly the disadvantages of independent enterprise, and sought to establish centralised industries working for the State. At that time, this amounted to a royal industry, contributing to the profit of the royal purse.

As far as arts and crafts were concerned, he tried to achieve his aim by founding an enormous manufactory, that included the tapestry industry among other crafts.

In 1667 the Gobelins workshop was named the *Manufacture royale des Meubles de la Couronne*. In view of the circumstances, it is not surprising that, especially in the first years, a large part of the products from this factory – tapestries in particular – found its way directly into the king's palaces, leaving little or nothing for other would-be purchasers.

Therefore other ateliers were set up also in Aubusson and Beauvais, in order to provide France with more tapestries. These tapestries in general were of considerably lower quality than the Parisian ones. In particular, they included smaller pieces such as chair covers.

As principal director of the Paris factory the king appointed Charles Lebrun. This was a man of universal talents: painter, sculptor, decorator and designer. The tapestries which now issued from the workshops so united structural features, ornament and the human figure that the *gobelins*, more than ever before, formed an integral part in the decor of the house where they hung.

Lebrun assembled a large staff of the most skilful cartoon-designers and operatives, each of whom was capable of executing almost completely a given part of the great whole.

Generally speaking, literature, in this century, was pretty well exhausted as a source of subjects for tapestries. Painting took its place. Indeed, the affinity between the two arts was already extremely close in former times, but there had been no talk of direct dependence. At the most, one might say painting possessed the rights of seniority.

Presently the tapestries were to become thoroughly dependent on pictures for their ideas, and soon they were even to be little more than copies.

But we have not yet arrived at this point.

For the time being, painting technique was moving further away from the principles that had prevailed up to now, and taking less account of the laws of the plane surface. And although the tapestry artists followed this trend at a distance, the decorative principle still sufficiently asserted its own value in company with colour and form.

Although the old religious themes and those borrowed from antiquity still continued to be used, next to these happenings of recent times filled an ever greater place on the tapestries. Important events like the destruction of the Armada appeared in the tapestries, with the help of expert designers and artists who specialised in these subjects.

Of course the mystery plays had long since disappeared, just as the stage performances that furnished material for sixteenth century tapestries. Now for choice they wove lighter subjects – and lighter colours – on the loom, such as scenes from Guarino's operas and pastorals like Ariosto's famous *Orlando Furioso*. Although such pieces saw the light in the previous century, they appeared in the tapestries only during the present one, thus furnishing a proof that the adoption of new ideas is a very slow process.

The art of tapestry taken as a whole, but with particular reference to the reign of Louis XIV, gives in this century a true reflection of the life of court society. Of great hunting parties in the style of the fifteenth century, there is no further mention.

The old, high nobility, once jealous to the death of a prince that they, as the highest class, acknowledged as their equal, had degenerated to a throng of periwigged, gold-embroidered, justaucorps-clad courtiers, who frittered their time in the salons of the royal palace among associates of their own kind.

The ballet and comedy of which we were speaking just now slowly but surely became more and more drawn towards country-life. Not infrequently the princes themselves would join in the play, and their courtiers acted as shepherds and shepherdesses.

No wonder that by and by these scenes were reproduced in the tapestries too. Fortunately, happenings of direct contemporary relevance continued to be included in the programme.

We cannot begin to enumerate the principal tapestries made in Paris. We wish to make one exception for those tapestries which have to do with the life of Louis XIV himself. This series comprises fourteen tapestries, of particular interest to the Dutch, since they depict Louis' acts of war against Holland. Various editions of this series were made.

The same applies to other famous sequences that could not be reproduced often enough, such as a series about Alexander, and a cycle of scenes from the life of Moses.

The Paris manufactory was at its zenith in the 'eighties. At that time, this establishment became an ever more popular meeting-place for all who had an interest in tapestry. Members of the highest lay and clerical classes could always be sure of encountering one or other of their friends, male and female, in these rooms.

The technical possibilities at that period were almost unlimited. The dyes were prepared and tested in their own laboratories. The thread shone magnificently and stayed in good condition for years. Silk, together with gold thread, was now widely employed. This was used above all to impart lustre.

Just as swiftly as the flowering came the decline. At the end of this century the factory was as good as abandoned, a number of the workers returning to Flanders, where they had come from.

2. Brussels

We too shall return to Brussels.

If we ask the cause of this sudden decline in Paris, then the answer must be – the revoking of the Edict of Nantes by Louis XIV in 1685 and financial stringencies caused by the war of the League of Augsburg. Many, including highly-skilled weavers, quitted the country in order not to get into difficulties.

Naturally, these people moved to the other great centres, including Brussels, where the skilful among them found no lack of work.

Competition among monarchs who desired tapestry workshops in their capitals at any price had become so great that they advanced substantial sums of money to the merchants to prevent their moving abroad.

Brussels held a strong position in the midst of this rivalry. The guild looking after the interests of the tapestryworkers was of such consequence that in 1655 it could even set up its own 'tapissers' bank. Here before long were lodged tapestries to the value of £15,000. Business to do with tapestries was transacted at this depository, and here the merchants could raise money on their security.

Just as in the sixteenth century, the Brussels trade in luxury tapestries was principally in the hands of a few wholesale dealers – the Reymbouts, the Reydams, the Leyniers and others.

A name of importance in this place, however, is that of a great Flemish painter, who like Raphael in the previous century, left his mark on the tapestries of his time. We refer to the artist Peter Paul Rubens, who in the year 1618 designed his first cartoon.

The space composition that Raphael had introduced by a lowering of the horizon in the picture was in its turn set at nothing by Rubens, who took the horizon as high as possible, almost lifting it out of the picture. We view the depicted scene as if it were enacted on a frieze. A further characteristic of the works designed by Rubens is the blending of the middleground with the frame.

However hackneyed we may consider the themes of such famous sequences as those on the life of Decius Mus or of Constantine, nevertheless these tapestries have an air of grandeur we cannot fail to recognise, and tower above the work of his contemporaries.

Rubens not only worked for the Spanish Archdukes in Brussels, but also for King Louis XIII of France and King Charles I of England.

After Rubens, the painter Jacob Jordaens and the Teniers family should be mentioned as important cartoon-designers.

In the last quarter of the seventeenth century, Brussels could not wholly resist the great influence emanating from Paris. Parisian gobelins were even imitated in Brussels.

The decline of the industry in Paris, however, was to give Brussels a new opportunity.

VI Tapestry in the Eighteenth Century

1. Paris

In 1695 the Gobelin factory was obliged to close its doors. In part this was a consequence of the war, but also it was partly due to the weavers' having moved out one after the other. The larger and richer princely courts of Europe now saw their chance and took advantage of it. They endeavoured to set up factories of their own by making favourable offers to the ambulant weavers.

Certain princes were successful in their efforts. Peter the Great of Russia and Frederick the Great of Prussia both established a modest industry.

But Paris was still far from being utterly defeated. After a few years, the abandoned looms were again set up in business and Paris could supply tapestries once more. So great was the success, in fact, that in the eighteenth century as well, this city would remain the centre of tapestry-weaving for the whole of France.

Once again, just as in former times, the luxury tapestries were made there, a number of them woven by the expensive high-warp process. Elsewhere, in such places as Aubusson and Beauvais, they made exclusively the cheaper qualities on the low-warp looms.

The character of the subjects on the tapestries, however, was again slowly changing. The antique and religious material that so long had taken pride of place, now at last dropped out of favour. Contemporary military achievements, however, remained in vogue. Together with these, landscape of course retained an important position, for that is precisely what was now asked of the tapestry artist – to ally himself with the painter in reproducing scenes from nature. Soon people were interested only in tapestries which looked like cleverly-imitated paintings, such as those made after paintings by Watteau. This artist was unable to exercise any personal effect on this development, for he died as early as 1721, but his pupils, who continued to paint in his style, spread his influence all the more zealously.

Pastoral scenes were still favoured. Once more, splendid sets of tapestries came from the looms.

Whatever may be said against the conceptions of the leading artists as applied to the realm of tapestry, the incomparable technical ability of the weavers always relegates such criticism to secondary importance.

The most celebrated masters of the palette guided the businesses in the capacity of directors. Here we shall only mention Jean-Baptiste Oudry and Jean François Boucher. The latter in particular was for the eighteenth century what Rubens

61

had been for the seventeenth and Raphael for the sixteenth: he originated and set the pace for a new trend.

In contrast with the monumental style of Lebrun – big figures in the foreground of the tapestry, wholly in the manner of painterly principles of those days – now we see perspective woodland views, in which the gaze loses itself in misty distances.

We have already indicated that at this time the technical principles of tapestry-weaving and painting eventually would become so much at odds that clashes were bound to occur. The very fact that the exemplars – the paintings – in the nature of the case do not readily lend themselves to monumental treatment as regards technique and dimensions, whereas the cartoons demand this monumental quality, was already furthering this conflict.

In addition to the themes already mentioned, fresh sources of inspiration were constantly being discovered. Cervantes' *Don Quixote*, written at the beginning of the seventeenth century, could now – its satire rendered harmless by the passage of time – make its contribution.

Towards the end of this rich development, the figures of the Italian *commedia dell' arte* also take their place, next to those of French comedy. After so many appearances on the boards, Harlequin and Pantaloon, Capitano, Scapino and Dottore now find their way on to the tapestry, there to repeat their performances.

Most of these tapestries too are purely pictorial in conception. Eventually the fables of La Fontaine were enthusiastically depicted, if not on the great tapestries then certainly on the chair covers.

The interest that Mme de Pompadour succeeded in arousing for the products of Chinese art was not only expressed in fabric patterns, but no less in the designs on tapestries. Everywhere these *chinoiseries* made their appearance.

The slow shift from the decorative to the illustrative only comes to a stop with the arrival of classicism. This trend was exemplified in the Gobelin factory by the designs of Jacques Louis David. The latter's linear-literary style ill agreed with the soft material with which the weaver works. Thus in his day one may observe a distinct deterioration in tapestries.

In 1790, in the days of the Terror, when Marat proposed to close the factory, this proposal it is true was rejected by the National Assembly out of a sort of patriotic pride in the old institution. But this only meant prolonging its life for a few years. As early as 1793 the demolition began.

Then tapestries depicting the life of Louis XIV were burned in Paris. When the following year the Committee of Public Safety opened the factory once again, all the Boucher tapestries still on the looms were nevertheless condemned. Napoleon's attempts to breathe new life into the business also miscarried, for when the Bourbons returned to power, all the scenes from the Emperor's life still in the making were in their turn pulled off the looms.

The old historical and religious themes did indeed recur yet again, but they aroused so little interest the factory languished accordingly. They managed as best they might, using sometimes extremely old cartoons from stock, until in 1871, at the rising of the communes, the factory was plundered and ruined. The whole stock of tapestries was destroyed.

Meanwhile, however, at the Great Exhibition in London in 1851, the seeds had already been sown for a promising future development.

2. Brussels

Brussels was undergoing a similar development.

Here too, fewer subjects were borrowed from ancient history, mythology and theology, but there remained an interest in contemporary military events. Splendid tapestries of this kind were still made, such as those designed after pictures by A.F. van der Meulen, a famous painter of battle scenes. Whether he himself worked on the cartoons cannot be ascertained, but his pictures were certainly copied without scruple by the pattern-designers.

This series was executed by the wholesale dealers who dominated the Brussels tapestry industry in this century – the De Vos family, mentioned as early as 1426, and the Van der Borghts, another ancient family. The draughtsmen and designers had obviously been inspired, as far as composition was concerned, by the series about Louis XIV's wars, which has already been mentioned.

But what a difference!

The tapestries from the Gobelin factory were rich in colour; those of Brussels were characterised by a marked preference for soft, brown-green tints in the rendering of background and

Brussels,
1528.

Florence, first half of the
seventeenth century.

Paris, first
half of the seven-
teenth century.

From left to right: Tournai, end of the sixteenth
century; Mechelen, first half of the sixteenth
century; Oudenaarde, mid-sixteenth century.

A·BAERT

Alexander Baert of Amsterdam. There were two weavers
of this name; the one worked
from 1698–1719, the other
from 1719–1752.

MANDER·
FECIT'AN'1619

Karel van Mander, active in Delft
from 1615–1623.

Pauwels Rombouts,
born 1579.

Willem Andriesz. de
Baet, 1541–1572.

FRANCISCVS·SPIRINGIVS

A ᛏᛉ ᒿ ARNOLDVS·SPIRINCIVS

Franciscus and Arnoldus Spierinck, who worked in Delft; the former from
1592–1630, the latter from 1621–1640.

Mark which authenticated tapestries from Mortlake in the first half of the seventeenth century.

VANDERGVGHT

Maximiliaan van der Gught, 1635–1689.

Martin Reymbouts, who worked in Brussels in the first half of the seventeenth century.

Willem Pannemaker, mid-sixteenth century, Brussels.

Above: Frans Geubels; below: Willem Geubels; both active in Brussels, mid-sixteenth century.

BᵂB PVD BORCHT

Pieter van der Borght, active in Brussels. The town's mark stands before his name. First half of the eighteenth century.

Anton Reyniers, second half of the sixteenth century, Brussels.

Fig. 22. Some marks of ateliers and tapissers.

Fig. 23. Map showing the principal centres of the tapestry art and the course of its development in Western Europe.

I. The most important centre lay in what is at present Belgium *and the* Franco-Belgian *frontier region; that is, the former Spanish Netherlands provinces that once belonged to the Dukes of Burgundy and passed under the dominion of the French kings. In this district tapestries were made in the following places: Brussels, Antwerp, Arras, Tournai, Lille, Douai, Valenciennes, Cambrai, Ghent, Oudenaarde, Mechelen, Enghien, Leuven, Tienen, St. Truyen, Bruges, Mons, Binche.*

In the course of the centuries, this region extended its influence to France, Holland England, North Germany, Italy, Spain and Denmark.

II. France, *where we note these centres of production: Paris, Tours (Touraine), Angers (not well-known as a weaving-town), Aubusson (Marche), Felletin (Marche), Charleville, Nancy and Beauvais. Of these, Paris was by far the most important, influencing in the seventeenth century the production centres in Touraine as well as in the Marche and Beauvais. Furthermore, France exercised influence beyond her frontiers, notably in the South-East German and Bohemian dominions (shown on the map by Prague), the Spanish Netherlands North Germany, Sweden and Russia.*

III. Germany. *As regards the art of tapestry, this country has borrowed more than she herself has given. In North and Central Germany, production was plainly under the influence of the Franco-Belgian frontier region, with the exception of Berlin, which in the eighteenth century was stimulated by Parisian industry. In South Germany and adjacent regions the case is rather more difficult. On the one hand, there are the districts bordering on South Austria, which bring a character of their own to the tapestries. Yet here too French influences had very probably been active. This region, shown on the map by Prague, in its turn exerted influence on South Germany and the German-Swiss areas. Within the German-speaking countries, we can distinguish the following centres (among which we include not only places where the work was done, but also those where important tapestries were preserved): South-East Germany with the adjacent Bohemia; Bamberg and Nuremberg, both under the influence of Prague. One may also distinguish as more or less independent: Strasbourg, Frankfurt-am-Main, Mainz, Mannheim, Cologne, Kassel, Hildesheim, Halberstadt, Quedlinburg. In the two last-named towns, extremely old tapestries are preserved. Further still: Leipzig, Schwerin, Berlin, Dresden and Sigmaringen.*

IV. Italy. *The tapestry-industry in this country was wholly under Flemish influence. Centres are: Ferrara, Mantua, Correggio, Milan, Florence, Urbino, Perugia, Todi, Rome, Turin, Naples, Venice, Ravenna (where extremely old examples of tapestries are to be found), Siena. Of these places, Ferrara and Florence were the most important, the latter supplying goods to Turin and Naples.*

V. Holland. *Here, everything in this field of art was owed to the Spanish Netherlands. As centres – not in order of importance – we mention: Haarlem, Amsterdam, Leyden, The Hague, Delft, Gouda, Utrecht, Middelburg, Bergen op Zoom and 's-Hertogenbosch.*

VI. England. *Likewise under Flemish influence. A well-known workshop existed at Mortlake, Surrey.*

VII. Spain. *Under Netherlands influence, but achieved importance only in the eighteenth century. Centres: Madrid and Pastrana.*

VIII. Denmark. *This country too was dependent on the Netherlands. Centre: Copenhagen.*

IX. Sweden. *This country, on the other hand, was much indebted to France, next to relations with the Dutch. Centre: Stockholm.*

X. Russia. *Russia too took part in the development of the tapestry industry of Western Europe chiefly through French influence. St. Petersburg became an eminent centre.*

trees. For that matter, all the Brussels tapestries from the middle of this century show a decided preference for the warm, soft tints, with a few touches of intenser colour by way of contrast.

The treatment of light in these tapestries is sublime, and the groups of trees and the cloud-masses are most picturesquely rendered.

Compared with the Parisian tapestries, they bear a wholly personal stamp. The borders, too, are different. In Paris, these were often embellished with arabesque designs, whereas in Brussels much use was made of an arrangement of military accoutrements. In both cities, these borders gave place to narrow frames that scarcely left room for the specific mark of the designer or tapisser. These marks or tokens served to place origin, quality and price above suspicion, but in practice they were occasionally put to somewhat questionable use. Those of popular masters were sometimes employed all too freely – which may be unorthodox, but is surely human. (Fig. 22.)

But to return once more to the Flemish colour-range. The delicate combinations of colour, the strongly illusionistic treatment of imagined landscapes with the picturesque groups of trees and cloud formations that surrounded the great festival-halls on every side, formed the ideal setting for the lords and ladies wearing the old-fashioned justaucorps or the modern *habit à la française* and soft-coloured dresses with wide panniers.

We must not be too surprised that in these very circles, the scenes made fashionable by the painters of the Teniers family – the well-known peasant scenes, portraying the life and labour of the working-classes – remained in favour to the last.

Brussels finally came to an inglorious end as one factory after the other shut its doors. The interest of the rising bourgeoisie already tended more towards chintz hangings and before long even to printed paper.

In 1781 there were but three looms in use, and when, in 1794, the last representative of the renowned Van der Borght family died, that signified the end of the tapestry industry in Brussels.

Up to the last, the Empress Theresa of Austria together with the Stadtholder Karel van Lotharingen had assisted the Van der Borghts. Göbel accurately calls attention to the fact that the art of tapestry in the Spanish Netherlands began with the arrival of the Burgundian house, and died when the Austrian hereditary lands had to make way for the United Belgian States in 1790.

Of the other Flemish centres such as Antwerp, Lille and Oudenaarde, only the last-named is memorable, largely for the handsome 'verdures' that continued to be made there after the decline of Brussels.

VII The Development of Tapestry in Germany, Italy, Spain, England, Scandinavia and Russia

No country in Western Europe can in any way compare with France and the Spanish Netherlands as far as the development of tapestry is concerned.

Although we may attempt to reconstruct the causes for this phenomenon, after the lapse of time there is little likelihood that we can account for it fully, because of lack of data.

However, in view of the fact that Flanders occupied an important position as large-scale manufacturer and exporter of fine woollen stuffs from Roman times and more than a thousand years onwards – it is quite certain that the potential conditions

---

Fig. 24. France, with names of places where tapestries may still be viewed. This map, (page 70), just as the one which follows, makes no claim to be complete.

Aix-en-Provence: episcopal palace; cathedral of St. Sauveur
Anet: castle
Angers: castle-museum of Anjou; cathedral
Arles: Réattu museum
Azay-le-Rideau: castle
Beaune: hospital; treasury of Notre Dame; municipal museum
Beauvais: cathedral
Besançon: museum of fine arts
Bourges: hôtel Jacques-Coeur; hôtel Lallement
Chambord: castle

Champs: castle
Chartres: municipal museum
Châteaudun: castle
Chaumont: castle
Chenonceaux: castle
Cheverny: castle
Dijon: museum of fine arts
Fontainebleau: castle
Fontaine-Française: castle
Guéret: municipal museum
La Chaise-Dieu: abbey of Saint Robert
Langeais: castle
La Villeneuve: castle

69

Le Harras-du-Pin

Le Mans: treasury of the cathedral; Notre Dame de la Couture

Le Puy-en-Velay: Crozatier museum

Lyon: museum of decorative arts; civic hospice; silk museum

Marseilles: Grobet-Labadie museum; Cantini museum

Maupas: castle

Montgeoffroy: castle

Narbonne: cathedral

Nice: museum of fine arts

Niort: museum of fine arts

Paris: Louvre museum; museum of decorative arts; Gobelin museum; museum du Petit Palais; Cluny museum; Jacquemart-André museum; Marmottan museum; museum of modern art; Carnevalet museum; museum of the Légion d'honneur, museum de la France d'outre-mer.

Pau: castle

Rambouillet: castle

Rheims: museum of fine arts; cathedral

Saint-Etienne: industrial arts museum

Saumur: castle; Notre Dame de Nantilly; Saint Pierre

Sens: cathedral treasury

Serrant: castle

St. Jean-Cap-Ferrat: museum Ile-de-France

Strasbourg: castle

Talcy: castle

Thorigny-sur-Vire: castle

Toulouse: cathedral

Valenciennes: museum of fine arts

Versailles: palace

Vitré: castle

for the development of the tapestry industry were in existence.

That this potentiality became reality, was owing to the richness and might of the reigning princely families. There could be no possibility of high achievement unless both the condition of long experience and that of princely power were fulfilled.

For all that, a few words should be said about the development in the other countries of Western Europe.

Germany

We shall begin with Germany, not because this country is any exception to the rule we have just laid down, but rather because there we can trace back the development furthest.

The oldest pieces, as we have seen, came from the nunneries, and so far as our knowledge extends we ought probably to consider these convents as the principal production centres of the Middle Ages.

Germany never achieved a concentration of capital, enterprise and labour such as were found in France and Flanders. The division of power under the numerous princes of the country in itself constituted an obstacle, from the start. Be that as it may, the convents in Bamberg, Regensburg, Nuremberg, Basle and Alsace probably produced a considerable number of tapestries.

These were always relatively small pieces, somewhat primitive in manner. They are predominantly altar frontals and dorsals for ecclesiastical use. Others were designed for use as wallcoverings above the benches in the living-quarters of castles.

The 'Wildeman' or rustic tapestries, which we have already mentioned, are also fairly characteristic of Germany and its neighbours to the south-east. Among German tapestries of the later Middle Ages we also discover the well-known kind where the scene is enclosed in great scrolls bearing proverbs. The inscriptions on these scrolls were generally rendered in verse.

The tapestry made in this country and its nearest neighbours from after the sixteenth century reflects the influence of the great western centres to such a degree that it possesses few personal characteristics.

Almost every small independent dukedom or principality in Germany had at some time in the seventeenth or eighteenth

Fig. 25. Map of the German-speaking Countries.
The rich collection of tapestries in the Bohemian countries has, since 1945, become the property of the Czecho-Slovakian State. The most important are housed in the Industrial Arts Museums in Prague and Brno, and also in the museums of Liberec and Bratislava. Important tapestries are also preserved in the archiepiscopal palace in Prague and the town hall at Bratislava.

Bamberg: *cathedral*
Basle: *historical museum*
Berlin: *State Industrial Arts museum; Emperor Friedrich museum*
Bern: *historical museum*
Breslau: *Schlesischer industrial arts museum*
Budapest: *industrial arts museum*
Charlottenburg: *castle*
Cologne: *industrial arts museum*
Copenhagen: *museum*

Cracow: *St. Katherine's church*
Delitzsch: *town hall*
Dresden: *art gallery castle*
Erfurt: *cathedral*
Flensburg: *museum*
Frankfurt-am-Main: *industrial arts museum*
Freiburg: *muenster*
Gelnhausen: *St Mary's church*
Gengenbach: *church*
Gotha: *ducal museum*

72

centuries a tapestry-workshop to gratify the pride of its prince. The most important workshop of the seventeenth century was that founded by the Duke of Bavaria at Munich in 1604, under the direction of Jan and Hans van der Biest from Enghien. It produced in the first half of the century some fine sets of 'Months', 'Seasons' and 'Grotesques', and the 'History of Otto von Wittelsbach' to glorify the House of Bavaria.

In the eighteenth century, the tapestry works of the German states were mainly under the direction and influence of French rather than Flemish weavers and designers. The Munich factory, which was to last into the nineteenth century, was revived under a succession of French directors. One of its main original products was the 'History of the House of Wittelsbach' made between 1732 and 1746. Existing French tapestries were much copied in this period. At Berlin the Barraband family, established there in 1699, made grotesques, chinoiseries and scenes from the Italian Comedy closely connected with designs used at Beauvais; and at Schwabach the main designs used by Jean Peux were also very close to Beauvais tapestries inspired by the grotesques of Jean Bérain. At Erlangen, too, Bérain designs were made, and a series of 'Elements' after the seventeenth century Gobelins tapestry of Le Brun.

Greifswald: university
Halberstadt: cathedral
Hamburg: industrial arts museum
Hannover: Welfenmuseum; Kestner-
  museum
Hildesheim: cathedral; Knochem-
  hauerambtshaus
Kassel: Landesmuseum
Kiel: museum
Klagenfurth: museum
Leipzig: industrial arts museum;
  town hall
Lüneburg: town hall
Maihingen: castle
Mainz: cathedral
Mannheim: castle
Meldorf: museum
Munich: national museum
Nuremberg: Germanic museum; Bava-
  rian national museum; St. Sebald;
  St. Lorenz

Potsdam: castle
Prenzlau: museum
Prague: (see note at head of this list)
Regensburg: town hall
Salzburg: cathedral
Schwerin: castle
Schleiszheim: castle
Sigmaringen: castle
Soest: town hall
St. Gallen: museum
Strasbourg: cathedral
Stuttgart: castle
Trier: provincial museum
Vienna: Hofburg museum
Xanten: cathedral
Zabern: St. John's
Zürich: Landesmuseum

Fig. 26. Italy.

*Bergamo: (Citta Alta) S. M. Mag-
    giore*
Como: cathedral
Ferrara: cathedral
*Florence: Pal. Vecchio; Galleria
    degli Uffizi; Academia di belle
    Arti; Museo Nazionale (Bargello),
    Pitti, palace; Museo Bardini and
    other museums*
Genoa: Pal. Bianco
Gries (near Bolzano)
Mantua: Pal. Ducale

*Milan: Museo Poldi-Pezzoli;
    Castello*
Naples: Museo Nazionale
Piacenza: cathedral
Pisa: Museo Civico
*Rome: Museo Vaticano; Castel St.
    Angelo; Pal. Doria*
Trente: cathedral
Trieste: cathedral
Turin: palace
*Venice: Museo St. Marco; Museo
    Civico Correr; Ca d' Oro and
    other palaces*
Vigevano: cathedral

There were many other small tapestry works, most of them relatively short-lived; some staffed by foreign weavers, some producing small indigenous hangings and cushion covers with stiff figures and flower forms.

Italy

As for Italy, in the course of the fifteenth century, Flemish and French tapestry-workers were summoned to the Italian courts, where they organised workshops. Evidently the many Italian princely families tried to follow the example of their rich and powerful Burgundian colleagues, but in this they were only briefly successful.

Various causes may be assigned for their failure.

Firstly, in every case foreigners had to build up the businesses with their own labour. Once these migrants moved away again, then the workshops perforce had to close down. Furthermore, there was little need for the Italian nobility to drape their houses in this manner to make them habitable. The warmer south did not call for woollen hangings on the walls. Also, it was difficult for these products that depended on a centuries-long experience in handling wool, to flourish here in a country where for everything silk was the preferred material.

The first to induce Flemish tapestry-weavers to visit Italy was the princely family of the Gonzagas of Mantua. This occurred as early as 1419. The d'Este family established a workshop at Ferrara in 1436; Pope Nicholas V encouraged the starting of a factory at Rome in 1455; and most of the other important Italian cities, Florence, Milan, Perugia, Venice and Siena had shortlived workshops in the fifteenth century,

Sometimes weavers would be brought to a town for the making of one set of tapestries only, as seems to have been the case at Vigevano, where between 1501 and 1507 Benedetto da Milano and his companions worked on a set of 'The Months' for Gian Giacomo Trivulzio. Of the more permanent sixteenth century establishments, the most successful were those at Ferrara, under the direction of Nicholas and Jan Karcher, and at Florence, where Cosimo I founded the Medici tapestry-works in 1546 with the aid of Jan Rost from Brussels and of Nicholas Karcher, who left the Ferrara works. Both of these factories had a considerable output, particularly that at Florence, which was to last until 1737.

The third most important factory in Italy was probably that

established at Rome by Cardinal Barberini some time before 1630, initially under the direction of Jacques de la Rivière (Jacopo della Riviera). It suffered a setback in 1644, when its patron went into exile on the death of his uncle Pope Urban VIII, but revived on his return to Rome in 1653. In 1663 a set of tapestries showing the life of Pope Urban VIII was begun.

In the eighteenth century, apart from the Medici Factory, the San Michele works at Rome founded by Clement XI in 1710, and factories at Turin and Naples, both of which gained in staff from the closing of the Medici factory in 1737, were the most prolific.

The subjects of tapestries made in Italy did not vary greatly from the well known themes offered by the Bible, by mythology and by classical history, together with the allegories of months and seasons, grotesques and commemorative subjects. The designs of these tapestries, however, unlike those of other countries where the workshops were run by foreign weavers, were not copied from or greatly influenced by foreign designs. Indeed, in the sixteenth century quite the reverse process was taking place, for it was Raphael's designs for the 'Acts of the Apostles' which led to the revolution in northern tapestry design, as has been shown in a previous chapter. The greatest Flemish designers, Van Orley, Coecke, Cocxie and Vermeyen were strongly influenced by the styles of Raphael and his pupils, and of the later Mannerists, while tapestries after paintings by Raphael, Giulio Romano and Mantegna were made and remade on the northern looms.

A few Flemish designers were probably employed in Italy: Jan van der Straaten, known as Giovanni della Strada or Stradanus, was working in Florence in the late sixteenth century. The majority of Italian tapestries, however, were by Italian designers, such as Salviati, Bronzino, Archimboldo, Alessandro Allori and Battista Dossi, all well known painters. Among the most beautiful sixteenth century tapestries were the months and grotesques made at Florence from designs by Francesco Bacchiacca; while the most successful seventeenth century designs were those by Pietro da Cortona to complete a series of a 'Life of Constantine' begun by Rubens.

Spain

This country also has been only of minor importance in the development of the tapestry industry.

This fact will surely arouse surprise in those tourists who, at the Prado in Madrid and elsewhere in Spain, have had the opportunity of acquainting themselves with the magnificent tapestries which still exist there in great number. These tapestries however are mainly of Flemish manufacture. Spain hardly needed a national manufactory while linked by the Hapsburg dynasty to Brussels and other towns where the industry flourished.

Later there were various abortive attempts to set up workshops in Spain under Flemish directors. François Tons was paid a subsidy for this purpose in the 1620's by the Duke of Pastrana. In 1694, Jan de Melter of Brussels wanted to set up a factory in Madrid, but the Spanish government was unable to accept his offer because of the cost involved.

It was not until 1720, during the reign of Philip V, that Spain acquired a lasting factory of her own.

A master from Antwerp, Jacob van der Goten, established himself in the Spanish capital. His family managed to hold their own there for a century. The tapestries from this factory included 'The Conquest of Tunis', a copy of the sixteenth century Brussels set designed by Vermeyen and woven by Willem Pannemaker. 'The Story of Telemachus' was woven after paintings by Houasse, and 'The Story of Don Quixote' was made from the cartoons of Andrea Procaccini. Procaccini himself came from the San Michele factory in Rome to be director of the Spanish workshop when it was moved to Seville for three years.

The Madrid factory of Santa Barbara was encouraged by Charles III, who came to the throne in 1759. Many tapestries were woven in the latter half of the century after paintings by Teniers, Jordaens and Wouwermans. In 1776 the painter Goya was commissioned to design cartoons depicting the life of the Spanish people, and he produced no fewer than 45 between 1776 and 1791. It is for those tapestries that the Santa Barbara works is chiefly remembered.

The Napoleonic wars interrupted the production of tapestries, and in the nineteenth century only copies and repairs were undertaken.

England

The many references to 'tapicers' in English documents of the

Middle Ages are no proof that there was a flourishing tapestry industry in England at that time, for 'tapis', 'tapices' and similar terms were not always specific in their meaning, nor were they always used consistently.

The first documented English tapestry works were those set up in the sixteenth century by a country gentleman, William Sheldon, on land at Barcheston in Warwickshire and at Bordesley in Worcestershire. Whatever tapestries may previously have been made in England, Sheldon considered those made at Barcheston to be the first; for in his will of 1569–70 he describes Richard Hyckes, whom he had placed in charge of the works, as "the only author and beginner of this Art within this realm". It is not known exactly when these works were established, but tapestries were being supplied from Barcheston in 1568.

The main output of the Sheldon works consisted of fairly small tapestry-woven articles, such as cushion covers, a valance for a bed, a cover for a Bible or even the cuffs of a pair of gloves. Few of the large tapestries, made as wall-hangings or to cover tables, have survived. The best known are the detailed tapestry maps of English counties, one set of which was made in 1588, bearing the signature of Richard Hyckes and the arms of William Sheldon's son Ralph.

Although the attribution to the Sheldon workshops of the seasons tapestries dated 1611 at Hatfield House is uncertain, the workshops may still have been in production in 1619. If they were, their more provincial output was then eclipsed by the establishment of a manufactory at Mortlake, near London, under direct royal patronage. James I granted privileges to Sir Francis Crane, who was to administer the works, and who undertook to bring weavers from abroad and to apprentice English boys to learn the art of tapestry-weaving. By 1620, according to a Netherlands agent in London, at least fifty weavers and their families had come to work at Mortlake. Among them was Philip de Maecht, who evidently left Paris, where his monogram appears on tapestries fom the Faubourg Saint-Marcel, to become the director of weaving at Mortlake.

Under Sir Francis Crane, until his death in 1636, the rich silk and gold tapestries produced were among the finest in Europe. The first sets made, nine tapestries of 'The Story of Vulcan and Venus' and twelve pieces of 'The Months' were based on Flemish cartoons of the sixteenth century; but in 1623 Francis Cleyn, who had previously been employed by Christian

IV of Denmark, was appointed designer at Mortlake. He designed two sets which became extremely popular and were copied many times, one of the story of 'Hero and Leander' and one known as 'The Horses', several loosely connected classical and mythological scenes all containing magnificent horses. Cleyn is also believed to have designed the set of 'The Five Senses'.

The most famous set of tapestries made at Mortlake was probably 'The Acts of the Apostles' after the designs by Raphael. In 1623 Sir Francis Crane acting on the instructions of the Prince of Wales sent to Genoa to buy the seven cartoons remaining of the original ten. They were copied several times at Mortlake, the first set being enhanced by fine borders long believed to have been designed by Van Dyck, but possibly by Cleyn.

Both as Prince of Wales and as King, Charles II was an enthusiastic patron of the Mortlake works. The first and finest sets of tapestries were made for him, some of them bearing his arms in the border. In 1673 he bought the manufactory from Crane's brother, and it became known as 'The King's Works'.

The great dependence of Mortlake on royal patronage and subsidies, in spite of the considerable number of secondary sets made for members of the Court or for general sale, meant, however, that the 'King's Works' declined with the King's fortunes. As the financial difficulties of the Crown increased, payment of the £ 2,000 annuity to the workshop ceased, and all profits from sales were unequal to the expenses involved. By 1645 the weavers had had to refuse a good commission from the Prince of Orange because they had not sufficient capital to set up the looms and work until the first payment should be due. The workshop did not shut completely, but the numbers of weavers there dwindled, and standards of work declined.

During the Commonwealth an attempt was made to revive the Mortlake works. New subjects were planned: a 'Story of Abraham' (see plate 7) and 'The Triumph of Julius Caesar' after the series of paintings by Mantegna. Tapestries of the latter, however, were not completed until after the Restoration.

From 1660 to 1703, the year in which it was officially closed, the Mortlake works came under a succession of governors, none of whom succeeded in making a profit. Independent workshops established in those years seem to have drawn off many potential Mortlake commissions. Except where tapestries bear a specific signature and locality, it is hardly possible to tell from existing tapestries whether they were made at Mortlake or not. For the independent workshops used Mortlake designs and the Mortlake mark of the shield with the cross of St. George. The set of Venus and Adonis tapestries for example, was probably made at Mortlake, but there is no proof of this.

During this period, many copies were made of earlier sets. William Benood, working at Lambeth, made several sets of 'Vulcan and Venus' and of 'The Horses'. His work was recommended in a letter by Sir Sackville Crowe, an ex-governor of Mortlake, as early as 1670. In the same letter Crowe vilified the work of another independent worker, Francis Poyntz, from whom the king had already bought two sets of tapestries. Poyntz was situated at Hatton Garden and connected with the Great Wardrobe. His signature appears on tapestries of 'The Playing Boys' and on two new designs, the sea battle of Solebay (1672), one set of which is now at Hampton Court, and a set of 'Kings and Queens', which included full-length portraits of Charles I and Henrietta Maria. Thomas Poyntz, who continued working after the death of Francis in 1685, is known to have made a set of 'Months'.

In 1685 the Great Wardrobe moved to Great Queen Street, Soho, where John Vanderbank worked until 1727, making, among other sets, 'Venus and Cupid' after Albani, and 'The Elements' after Le Brun. His best known tapestries are probably the quaint 'Indian' and 'Chinoiserie' designs.

Other independent eighteenth century tapestry workers were Joshua Morris, George Smith Bradshaw, Paul Saunders and Stephan de May, of whom little more than their names and a few of their tapestries are known. In the 1750's there was a short-lived factory at Fulham set up by two Frenchmen to make tapestries and carpets.

The nineteenth century saw two main tapestry-weaving establishments in England. The first was at Windsor, where faithful and rather dull reproductions of paintings and engravings depicting mainly historic or contemporary events were made. The second was at Merton Abbey under the direction of William Morris. Using sometimes his own designs, sometimes those of Burne-Jones or of other Pre-Raphaelite friends, Morris attempted to restore tapestry-weaving as a distinctive decorative art rather than a mere imitation of painting. In some tapestries, such as the 'Angeli Laudantes', he revived the use of the 'millefleur' ground, which had not been used since the early sixteenth century. The return to vigorous hatching in place of the more

80

9. a. Hero mourning over Leander, from a set telling the story of Hero and Leander. Mortlake, between 1623 and 1636. b. Jason cutting down the Golden Fleece. Gobelin, dated 1761.

10. Tapestry with a pastoral scene – shepherds and shepherdesses playing on a swing. Eighteenth century.

11. Sheldon; early seventeenth century. A valance for a bed, showing hunting scenes.

12. *Soho; late seventeenth or early eighteenth century. A chinoiserie tapestry signed by John Vanderbank.*

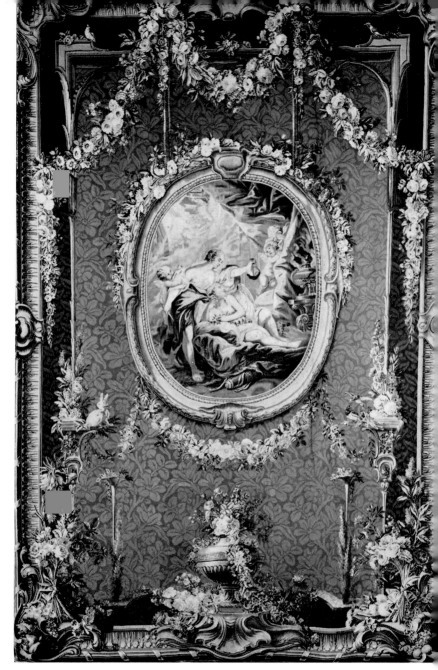

13. Cupid and Psyche. Eighteenth century.

14. Diana with hunting trophy. Eighteenth century.

15. *a.* 'L'Homme' – *design by Jean Lurçat, modern French tapestry-designer (born 1892). b. Theseus' battle with the Minotaur by Marc Saint-Saëns.*

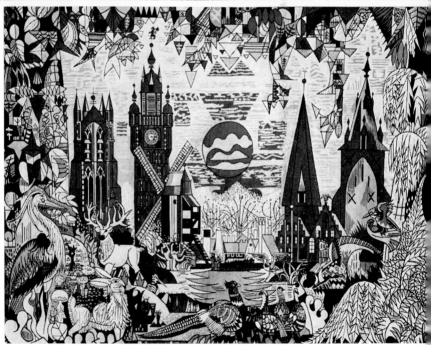

16. Two modern tapestries. a. 'La Terre' (1939). b. Autumn (1940). Both tapestries by Marcel Gromaire (born 1892).

painterly shading of colours previously in vogue may be said to have led the way for the bold designs of twentieth century tapestries.

Scandinavian Countries

When the church at Baldishol in Norway was pulled down in the 1880's, a piece of tapestry which probably dates from the beginning of the thirteenth century was discovered. Originally the long strip of tapestry was decorated with an arcade, in each arch of which stood a figure representing a month of the year. Only two figures, for the months of April and May, remain: a man in a long fur robe and a warrior on horseback. As their costume had features that are specifically Norwegian, it has been assumed that the tapestry was made in Norway. It is now in the Kunstindustrimuseum, Oslo.

No Scandinavian tapestries are known to survive between the Baldishol tapestry and those of the sixteenth century. By that time, the ruling monarchs had imported both tapestries and weavers from Flanders and the northern Netherlands, so tapestries produced thereafter were of three different types; the purely Scandinavian, mostly small hangings or cushion covers such as those woven in the Gudbrandsdalen district of Norway; the purely Flemish in inspiration, for example, the fine Swedish tapestries of the 'Story of David' made under Nils Eskilson at Kalmar before 1561; and the hybrid tapestries in which figures and border designs borrowed from other countries were transformed into the geometric patterns of native Scandinavian weaving.

Workers from the Netherlands are known to have been in Sweden as early as 1540. In Denmark, a set of tapestries showing the Kings of Denmark was made at Elsinore under the direction of Hans Knieper from Antwerp, around 1583.

Later, the royal Copenhagen tapestry works benefited from French aid and inspiration; the Barrabands of Aubusson being there in the second half of the seventeenth century, and François Léger working there between 1736 and 1744. The Swedish works centered in and around Stockholm were similarly devoted to imitations of the French style.

Russia

Peter the Great's emulation of the monarchs of Western

Europe made him also desire a royal tapestry works. It began with the establishment of French weavers at St. Petersburg in 1716, and the first tapestries made were copies of a Gobelins set of 'The Indies', which had been presented to the Tsar in Paris. In 1720, however, most of the French weavers left Russia, and the Russian weavers whom they had trained took over the work. With various later importations of foreign workers, the factory continued until about 1859, the most interesting of its productions being some very fine portraits of the Russian nobility.

VIII Tapestry in the Netherlands

One might say the Spanish Netherlands were predestined for the tapestry industry. Wool and linen – the materials required – were to be found there from early times. The Romans ordered their Atrebatic or Nervian woollen cloaks from these parts. Raw materials for dyes were also present, and any further requirements could be imported from abroad.

Century after century, skilful artisans took these materials in hand and worked them up into textiles of all sorts – cloth, lace, ribbons and so on.

This course of affairs fostered the rise of wholesale trade and the necessary concentration of capital. Here in Flanders, by the late Middle Ages a sharp division had already come about between the interests of this expanding, large-scale capital and the masses of working people in the towns. As usual, the great port of Antwerp on the Scheldt led the way.

The workman of former times, a respected craftsman given protection by his guild, was slowly but surely pushed out of the position he had won for himself, to become a wage-earner and nothing more. That is to say, he became defenceless against economic recession.

Now when the Flemish tapestry industry, through causes already mentioned, was confronted suddenly with an unexpected chance of expansion, large-scale capital also leaped upon such opportunities of making money. Around the 'thirties of the sixteenth century, in a relatively small town like Oudenaarde, more than 12,000 people were earning their bread, directly or indirectly, through this business.

Splendid in one way – since the need for labour and materials affected a wide stretch of country, and all shared in the prosperity to a modest extent – but deplorable in another, for ever larger numbers of workpeople became directly dependent on factors wholly indifferent to their true interests, and lost all influence on the international development of a luxury industry extremely sensitive to outside repercussions.

In Holland, however, by the sixteenth century matters were entirely different. People derived their income much more from shipping and farming, and less from industry, than in Flanders. Here too, of course, flax was grown and wool woven into cloth, but to a much more modest degree than in the Spanish Netherlands. Above all, north of the Rhine and its tributaries, the sharp social conflicts between capital and labour which already had caused so much unrest were as yet unknown.

Such conditions as obtained in Flanders for the development of a tapestry industry were here much less in evidence. This of course is not to say that here and there one might not have come across a single tapestry-weaver or so, come north for private reasons, but such exceptions had no effect worth mentioning on the general development of the tapestry industry.

That leading tapestry merchants eventually established themselves in Holland was the outcome of accidental circumstances rather than deliberate choice in the expectation of financial gain.

The settlement came about chiefly as a reaction to the persecution of Protestants in Flanders. The first edicts, appearing in 1529 and 1531, against the new doctrine, were already enough inducement for some to leave their homes. But the first great migration northward occurred when, under Philip II, from 1567 to 1570 more stringent edicts were proclaimed, and many Protestants moved out to those countries where they could practise their religion unhindered.

Among these refugees were many tapestry-workers. The subordination of the provinces in the Spanish Netherlands to Philip II, after the Union of Arras in 1579, once more caused many artisans and merchants, Protestant and Catholic alike, to move north. The Spanish Fury, when Antwerp was sacked by

Spanish soldiers who, among the rest of their plundering looted the entire stock of tapestries, did the rest. The war was depopulating Flanders.

The inhabitants of Antwerp were reduced to extreme poverty.

Who in those parts still had time to think about buying tapestry? People in the north were active in the fight for liberty. Perhaps there a new way of life could be built up.

The migration went on until well into the seventeenth century. While in Flanders the land became depopulated, over in the north, towns were having to extend their walls as fast as they could to make room for new inhabitants. This commercial prosperity must have roused golden hopes in the tapestry-workers from south of the great rivers.

Were these expectations to be fulfilled? The answer, generally-speaking, is no. Prosperous though they were, the inhabitants of the Seven Provinces united in the Netherlands were burgesses who lived not in palaces but in middle-class homes. They were not the sort to spend money on a whole series of splendid but bulky and costly tapestries which they would have to store away for lack of room. An occasional well-to-do private person might have made a purchase now and then, but these sales were of little significance. For the most part it was only such important institutions as the Boards of Admiralty, a few well-endowed hospices and universities, and the States and Councils of the provinces that could permit themselves such luxury. And even so, they were not making such purchases all the time. On the contrary, all was managed with frugality. For example, when we hear of such great bodies as the States General commissioning a work, more than likely it was in order to have a suitable present handy at need, than to adorn their own meeting-hall. Indeed, many official commissions of this sort were really a last attempt to get an extra profit from an investment made in some tapestry enterprise.

Even the princes of the House of Orange, though among the best clients, had to be thrifty in their purchases.

The tapestries most popular and easy to sell in these northern provinces, were smaller pieces like tablecloths, counterpanes, runners for chimneypieces, simple hangings, chair covers and cushions – but cushions above all.

The frugal Dutch of those days, when there was particular need of large tapestries for occasions such as state receptions, ceremonial processions, or at special events like the signing of a peace, used to hire them from the tapestry merchants.

With matters standing thus, it is not to be wondered at that tapestry-makers combined with their proper trade a business in such related articles as floor-carpets and so on.

As Dr G. F. van Ysselstein says in her *History of Tapestry-Making in the North Netherlands*: "this story is one of exiles whose profession slowly perishes".

The chief places where we know with certainty of tapestry-weaving establishments are, from south to north, Middelburg, Delft, Gouda, Utrecht, Amsterdam and Haarlem.

We will try in a few words to show what happened to these emigrant businesses.

Middelburg

A certain Jan de Maecht settled himself here in 1592, after the town council had made many fruitless attempts to encourage tapestry workers to move in. This De Maecht was a native of Brussels, but had already worked in Delft before he arrived in Middelburg. The town placed an abandoned monastery at his disposal.

We know of him that he made a part of a series of six tapestries depicting the victories of the Zealanders over the Spaniards. De Maecht and after him his two sons made for this series the 'Battle of Zierikzee', the 'Battle of Rammekens', the 'Battle of Lillo' and the 'Battle of Veere'. The tapestry of the 'Battle of Bergen (op Zoom)', also belonging to this series, was made by Spierinck of Delft. The marine-painter Vroom made the designs for these tapestries.

De Maecht's business kept going, with an interruption of a few years, until 1631.

Delft

Towards the end of the sixteenth century various masters from the south came to this place – the residence of the Princes of Orange during the struggle for freedom against Spain – to try their fortunes.

Chief among them was François Spierinck, from Antwerp. In his former home he seems to have been a distinguished man,

Fig. 27. *North and South Netherlands.*

Spanish Netherlands

The principal places in Belgium and the Franco-Belgian frontier region where tapestries have been made are shown on the map. In most of these, tapestries may be seen in the museums and churches. In particular, however, we would mention:

Beloeil: castle

Bergen: treasury of the St. Waudru

with a flourishing business. Here in Holland, too, he showed no intention of becoming a back number.

We know that he not only maintained connections over the whole of Holland, but also in the Scandinavian countries, Germany and England. Commissions came from every side, quite as much from the States of Zealand and the States General, as from abroad. For the commander of the English fleet, Lord Howard, he made a series of tapestries depicting the victories of the English over the Spanish Armada, these designs also being made by the painter Vroom. He supplied Gustavus Adolphus, King of Sweden, as well as the French nobility.

This flourishing business eventually came to grief through financial and internal difficulties. The latter began when the talented cartoon-designer Karel van Mander, who had worked for Spierinck, set up on his own, with financial backing from others.

Van Mander did splendid work, not least for King Christian of Denmark, to whose castle in Fredericksborg he delivered twenty-two tapestries. His financial problems, however, were not resolved when he died in 1623.

His weavers, tapestries and designs all went back to the ateliers of Spierinck, which continued to do good business after Van Mander's death. Financial difficulties occurred, nevertheless. By 1636, Aert Spierinck, one of François's sons, was described as 'former master tapisser', so must already have disposed of the business.

Bruges: pottery museum; St. Salvator
Brussels: museum Cinquantenaire; town hall; St. Goedele
Gaasbeek: castle

Ghent: museum of fine arts
Leuven: the 'Van der Kelen-Mertens' museum; St. Pierre
Tournai: cathedral

Holland

Amsterdam: Rijksmuseum
Arnhem: municipal museum
Bergen op Zoom: museum
Delft: Prinsenhof; museum Lambert van Meerten
Dordrecht: museum
Enkhuizen: town hall
Gouda: town hall; municipal museum
Groningen: antiquarian museum
Haarlem: town hall; Frans Hals museum
The Hague: municipal museum

's-Hertogenbosch: town hall
Kapelle: town hall
Leeuwarden: Frisian museum
Leyden: Museum De Lakenhal; St. Annahofje
Maastricht: town hall
Middelburg: abbey courthouse
Nijmegen: town hall
Rotterdam: municipal museum
Schoonhoven: town hall
Utrecht: Bartholomeusgasthuis

87

Next to the Spierinck family, that of Van der Gught deserves mention. This family too had dealings with many princes, and supplied tapestries to Prince Frederick Henry among others. They also did work for Queen Christina of Sweden, in partnership with tapestry-workers from Delft and Gouda. A member of this family also supplied tapestry to the towns of Delft and Utrecht and – much later – yet more tapestry, this time for the Aldermen Room of the new Town Hall at 's-Hertogenbosch.

The work of their atelier is the finest done in Holland.

Gouda

Exiles from the south settled in this town, too, both before and after the fall of Antwerp. Tapestry-workers from Oudenaarde established themselves in Gouda after the Spanish Fury.

Among designers connected with the tapestry industry in the sixteenth century, we meet first of all the famous family of Crabeth, glass-painters celebrated for the splendid windows in Gouda's Great Church.

Little, however, is known of the actual tapestry workshops of the time. The most important atelier was owned by a certain Jan Rufelaar, who carried on business towards the end of the sixteenth and the beginning of the seventeenth century. He manufactured many small articles, such as armorial tapestries, table covers, 'verdures' and cushions.

In Gouda we come across the names of many craftsmen, but no outstanding man of business, such as Aert Spierinck in Delft.

The name of Abraham Adriaansz Goossensom deserves mention, as director of one of the town's largest ateliers. He collaborated with Van der Gught of Delft in furnishing tapestries for Sweden.

Tobias Schaep, who also owned an atelier in Gouda, made a series of 'The Life of Christ' for a Swedish client between 1634 and 1637, the year of his death.

There is alas but little work surviving that may with confidence be attributed to the Gouda masters.

Utrecht

Only smaller businesses were established here, specialising in cushions and other tapestries of small dimensions.

Amsterdam

The same also applies, remarkably enough, to most of the businesses in Amsterdam.

One would have expected Amsterdam, which flourished so vigorously after the fall of Antwerp, to have taken a great part in tapestry-weaving, but this apparently did not occur. Like Antwerp itself, Amsterdam played a more important role in the transit trade, rather than in the manufacture of tapestries. In the second half of the sixteenth century, what we read about the work of tapissers always concerns the delivery, repair and cleaning of cushions.

Betweeen 1620 and 1630, a certain Joris Nauwinck was in business on a larger scale, and as well as supplying tapestries to the 'Illustre School' at Utrecht, even sold his goods abroad.

Then there was the De Cracht family, better known as merchants than weavers. Related to the Nauwinck family, they too furnished many tapestries to foreign princes, including the Elector Frederick William II of Brandenburg. William II, Prince of Orange, received from them a series of nineteen landscape pieces for the great hall of the Noordeinde Palace in The Hague.

Two sons continued the business in 1662.

Still later in Amsterdam we come across Alexander Baert. A native of Oudenaarde, he had worked in Gouda while waiting for business premises to become available in Amsterdam. But his first deliveries of tapestry in Amsterdam bring us already to the beginning of the eighteenth century.

Thus this town took hardly any part in the tapestry industry until the years of decline, and then on a modest scale. Besides his business in Amsterdam, this Baert took the opportunity to open a branch establishment at The Hague. The workshops in Amsterdam functioned until the second half of the eighteenth century.

Schoonhoven

This little town also played a modest role in the tapestry industry. Joris Nauwinck, already mentioned as a merchant in Amsterdam, was working there from the beginning of the seventeenth century. The Town Hall of Leyden, among others, was provided with his tapestries. One Franz Guys is later mentioned as being employed there.

The Hague

There were certainly tapestry workshops active in The Hague, but as branches of businesses established elsewhere.

Thus we come across the names of Abraham Goossensom, the Van der Gughts, and the Baerts, all suppliers of tapestry who were manufacturing in other places.

Haarlem

A few tapestry-workers carried on their trade in this town, too. Once more, we come across names met with elsewhere. However, in the first half of the seventeenth century Joseph Thienpondt was working independently. From his atelier came the tapestry dated 1629 depicting the capture of Damietta by the Crusaders – a tapestry still to be seen in the council room at the Town Hall.

We hear also of tapestry-workers in Rotterdam, Leyden, Dordrecht, 's-Hertogenbosch and Leeuwarden. But nowhere was business carried on with a vigour that even remotely resembles that of the towns in the Spanish Netherlands.

Here it is well to recall that the refugees were not everywhere received with open arms. People saw them, not always without reason, more as potential rivals than as victims of religious persecution. Men in places like Leyden and South Beveland, where a flourishing textile industry already existed, would not exactly have made it easy for newcomers in a similar line of business.

Here too the supply of skilled labour was limited, and, unlike the south, people had not worked at the trade for generations.

There was no lack of hard work. We read of cartoon-designers employed at a daily wage, who, in summertime, worked from daybreak for as long as they could see, each and every day. There is no reason to suppose the working-day of the weavers was any shorter, especially when we remember that the employers almost literally fought each other for the available supplies of labour.

To review the situation as a whole, it should be said that the emigrants, with the means at their disposal, produced good work in the current fashion in Holland.

90

This is particularly true of the historical pieces, depicting battles and sieges on land and sea.

The influence of a peculiarly Dutch genre is to be seen in tapestries with geographical details and plans of towns – subjects which to our view lend themselves extremely well to the purpose.

Of the historical pieces and plans of towns, we will mention only the 'Siege of Leyden in 1574' – after the map by Hans Liefrinck – made by Lanckeert in Delft; the six victory tapestries of the Zealanders already referred to; a series by Thienponts showing the history of Haarlem, and tapestries depicting the destruction of the Armada, and the battle of Nieuport, made on the looms of François Spierinck at Delft.

IX The Renaissance in the Present Century

If in our own days interest has again been awakened in this noble and ancient handwork, then this may with justice be styled a re-birth, a true renaissance. At the end of the previous century, it seemed as if the role played by the tapestry had died out. People were no longer aware of the lofty place it once had occupied, and with that all appreciation had vanished. Apparently, they were blind even to the intrinsic beauty of the old pieces.

It is common knowledge that, in the first half of the nineteenth century, old tapestries into which much gold thread had been woven were pulled to pieces without further consideration, merely for the commercial value of that gold.

The former owners of the costly pieces perhaps had perished in the years of the Terror in France, or, driven out of their estates, had died in exile. Their heirs, frequently involved in financial difficulties, could sometimes do no other than sell to the highest bidder.

91

Dr G. F. van Ysselstein records in her book several events which plainly reveal how little respect was shown for the old fabrics. About the year 1840 a set of magnificent tapestries made in Tournai was discovered doing duty in a stable to keep out the draught, while in 1860 a tapestry that once had hung in the Town Hall at Haarlem was found screening plants in a nurserygarden.

Other melancholy examples could easily be cited.

Notwithstanding this debasement, the industry as such did remain in existence here and there, but from the artistic point of view there was no possible comparison with earlier times.

The general revival of industrial art after the Great Exhibition in London in 1851 brought about a change in the situation. At this exhibition for the first time on a large scale, not only products of the western countries but also those of the east were brought before the eyes of the public – and of the artists.

The reactions of the two groups differed widely.

The general public was more than ever convinced by this exhibition of the high level of industrial achievement, but the artists thought otherwise about it. Among those who could not shut their eyes to the decadence of industrial art standards in the western world of those days, we ought specially to mention the German Gottfried Semper, an architect who lived and worked in London from 1848. He was supported in his endeavours to raise standards by, among others, the English philosopher, John Ruskin. In the second half of the century William Morris attempted to improve textile design in general and made new tapestries, as has been mentioned.

In France, Viollet-le-Duc pursued similar objectives. Holland followed this development from afar. Here too, appreciation of good building as well as industrial art had sunk to a deplorable level.

There was one who did protest. This man was Jhr. Victor de Stuers, who, in his pamphlet *Holland op zijn smalst* recalled the Government to its obligations.

His activity bore fruit. For, after the example of similar measures already furnished by England, France and other western European countries, the Government began, on the one hand, to concern itself with education in the arts and crafts, and on the other, with the establishment of a great national museum. Slowly, interest in the old, half-forgotten techniques revived.

At first, only a few artists recognised the latent possibilities that still existed in the art of tapestry, and attempted new ventures on the old looms. In Holland, Lion Cachet and Willem van Konijnenburg deserve mention. In Sweden, the brunt of the struggle was borne by Alf Wallender, Ferdinand Boberg and Agnes Branting.

In Norway, new workshops for tapestry were set up under the auspices of the 'Norske Husflidforeninge'. A leading artist here was Gerhard Munthe. Sweden wished to follow Norway's example, but first came the rude shock of finding that the very principles of the technique had to be learned afresh. In Austria and Germany, too, new centres came into existence here and there, influenced by young artists.

But it was France that led the vanguard. There the old industry had never wholly died. A few ateliers had kept on working as best as they might, under heavy competition from products made on the Jacquard machine, and from printed textiles.

Here again, the young artists took up the old craft once more and managed to impart a new significance to it, especially in Paris and Aubusson. We shall only mention the name of Boutet de Monvel. He and others with him, inspired by recent ideas in the advertising art of their day, were to give fresh impulses to the art of tapestry.

After the Gobelin factory in Paris, Aubusson deserves special mention as the centre from which the world was again to be supplied with tapestries. It is not wholly fortuitous that a new development should begin from this place. Aubusson lies on the banks of the little river Creuze, and, in contrast with most French rivers, the water of this stream apparently is exceptionally good for use in wool-dyeing.

The artist Jean Lurçat, for many years now the president of the international tapestry centre at Aubusson, had breathed new life into the industry there. At the moment of writing, there are seven workshops active, the designs for their tapestries being provided by various artists.

Lurçat himself usually makes large tapestries on a dark, often black, background. His subjects vary widely, but are always fantastic. He likes to make up a composition around an animal – a cock or a fish, for example – but also uses plant motifs, such as grapes. Further subjects relate to poetry, the victory of peace, the horror of war, and so on. He uses few but bold colours, linked together by the dark background.

Under his direction, work is carried out, just as formerly, from full-size designs on cardboard or board. A skilled worker in his ateliers, it appears, may produce about a square yard per month.

On the site of what was once the world-famed manufactory, but where today the Gobelin museum is housed, tapestries are again being made after designs of progressive artists. In contrast with Lurçat's work, which may scarcely be called modern any longer by today's standards, Jean Deyrolle and Passinos produce extremely modern, abstract compositions.

Other countries too are actively engaged in rebuilding the industry.

As for Germany, already during the Nazi era, tapestries were being made for public buildings. The great majority of these fabrics, however, are satisfying neither artistically nor in subject-matter. Since that time, however, the spirit of the land has changed.

The well-known American magazine *Time*, in the number for August 1962, noted that at present tapestries are being made in pretty well every country in Europe. It went on to remark that, in many ateliers, the tapissers are once more working elbow to elbow and plying their shuttles just as in former times.

Interest has become so widespread that in Lausanne, Switzerland, in the previous year, it was possible to mount an international exhibition of modern tapestries. On view was the work of fifty-seven artists from seventeen countries, from both sides of the Iron Curtain, and from America as well as Japan. Owing to the space available, each artist was allowed to contribute only one piece of work. One exception was made: Matisse, in view of his pioneering labour in this field, was given leave to exhibit two pieces.

Not only new themes, but new techniques also, were to be seen. The Japanese contribution in particular aroused astonishment – aesthetic as well as technical.

Young artists have not been alone in their efforts to further the revival of the art of tapestry, which has had the support of older artists, such as Picasso, as well. The architect Charles Eduard Jeanneret, better known as Le Corbusier, designs tapestries.

Among the younger artists, we must mention the Belgian, Mary Dambiermont, and Lilly Keller of Switzerland, and also the Polish Ada Kierzkowska, whose designs show some resemblance to the work of Miró, the Spanish surrealist painter.

As regards Holland: after the forerunners to whom we have already called attention, the most noteworthy artist is perhaps

Christaan de Moor. At the invitation of the Dutch government, he, together with Bouhuys, Kupershoek, Roelofs, Van der Steene and Andree, executed a series of tapestries concerning the parable of the Prodigal Son, each artist designing a single tapestry.

Lex Horn, too, is known for his pioneer work in this field.

That Belgium, the old nucleus of the tapestry art, should not lag behind, will surprise nobody. Here, for that matter, just as in France, the looms were never wholly idle – although perhaps it's better not to enquire too closely into details.

Here the growing interest may be witnessed in the publication of the magazine *Artes Textiles* and in the renewed activity of very old ateliers such as in Mechelen.

Of course, this revival of interest has brought home the need for experts to restore neglected tapestries. Therefore a few words should also be said on this subject. Obviously, in the repair of pieces of any value, expert assistance is indispensable. Here follow only a few general hints.

Dirty tapestries ought first to be washed – that is, if their condition will still allow this treatment. (In case of doubt, first consult an expert.) No wringing or stretching in the wash, of course – think of the warp! It is naturally highly inadvisable to tackle dirty pieces with caustic substances. For example, you can never tell how the colours will react.

The insertion of new warp threads in a damaged part is decidedly work for the professional. It is clearly something more difficult than darning a hole in an old bit of knitting, albeit in principle there is something in common.

In mending damaged portions, ought one to look for the original colours, as far as possible, or should one rather match the colours according to their state at the moment? The latter may give immediate satisfaction, but the first method is still to be preferred with a view to the future.

It is self-evident that all old tapestries, let us say from the seventeenth and eighteenth centuries, will have suffered more or less from the ravages of time. Colours in particular will no longer look like new. Indeed, if they do, some suspicion of the authenticity may well be warranted. In this respect as in others, the human mind has not proved barren in devising means of passing off new for old. In some cases, there may not be a single old thread. Others have been reconstructed on the remains of a genuine old piece. That lends an air of distinction.

That there are also 'afsetters' – retouchers – still busy today is not improbable. It is easy to falsify by means of paint, even water-paint.

When buying a costly piece (generally to be procured only through bona-fide dealers) the advice of an expert is clearly desirable.

The fact that in most old tapestries centrepiece and border can easily become separated from each other, has of course also given rise to impostures. Repeatedly, centrepieces without borders and borders without centrepieces have been united, though perhaps this can scarcely be styled an evil.

When judging old tapestries, we ought also to bear in mind that in the course of the years the colours have altered in relation to each other. The yellow element in green dyes will largely have faded, and the blue therefore will have become stronger than the artist originally intended. This phenomenon can be particularly observed in the 'verdures' that were made in Aubusson and Oudenaarde.

Finally, anyone seeking information and help in these matters can find guidance in Holland at the workshop for the restoration of antique textiles – where many sadly-neglected tapestries have already been repaired in a thoroughly responsible manner.*

X Favourite Subjects for Tapestries

In the Fourteenth and Fifteenth Centuries
I. Relating to ancient history and mythology
The deeds of Alexander the Great.
The siege of Troy.
The story of Aeneas.

---

* Leidseplein 36; Haarlem, Holland.

The labours of Hercules:
  a. the slaying of the Nemean Lion;
  b. the battle with the nine-headed Lernaean Hydra;
  c. the taking of the Ceryneian Hind with the golden horns
  d. the capture, alive, of the Erymanthian Boar;
  e. the cleansing of the Augean stables;
  f. the driving away of the Stymphalian Birds;
  g. the fetching of the Cretan Bull;
  h. the taking of the Wild Horses of Diomedes;
  i. taking possession of the girdle of Hippolyte, Queen of the Amazons;
  j. the seizing of the Cattle of Geryon;
  k. fetching the Golden Apples of the Hesperides;
  l. the capture of Cerberus, the Hound of Hell;
Caesar and Pompey.
The conquest of Thebes.
The life of Augustus.
Jason and the Golden Fleece.
Virgil's history.

II. Relating to the Early Middle Ages
The deeds of Charlemagne.
The exploits of William of Orange.
The quest for the Holy Grail.
King Arthur and the Knights of the Round Table.
The story of St. George.
The story of Lancelot.
The story of Lohengrin.
The story of Tristan and Iseult.
Parsifal.
Stories of Mohammed.

III. Relating to the Crusades
The history of Cyprus.
The story of Richard Coeur de Lion.
The story of Geoffrey de Bouillon.

IV. Contemporary Events
The story of Bertrand du Guesclin.
The siege of Liège in 1488.
The battle of Roosebeke in 1382.
Stories concerning the Great Khan – probably in connection with the travels of Marco Polo in the Far East.

V. General

Tapestries representing deeds of heroes and heroines.

VI. Religious Themes

The story of Jesus.

The story of the Virgin Mary.

Stories from the Old Testament – among others those of David, Jephthah, Samson and Esther.

Stories taken from the Apocrypha:

    a. Susanna and the Elders;

    b. Judas Maccabeus;

    c. the story of Judith.

Traditional stories:

    a. the Empress Helena and the finding of the True Cross;

    b. representations of the Sibyls. Usually they are portrayed in the following manner:

    1. the Persian Sibyl with a monster at her feet and a lantern in her hand;

    2. the Libyan Sibyl holding a candle;

    3. the Erythraean Sibyl with a flower;

    4. the Cummaean Sibyl with a golden dish;

    5. the Cimmerian Sibyl with a horn of abundance;

    6. the Samian Sibyl with a cradle;

    7. the European Sibyl armed with a sword;

    8. the Tiburtine Sibyl with a severed hand beside her;

    9. the Agrippine Sibyl holding a scourge;

    10. the Delphic Sibyl with a crown of thorns;

    11. the Hellespontine Sibyl carrying a great cross;

    12. the Phrygian Sibyl with the cross of victory;

    c. Representations relating to the so-called Vengeance of the Saviour, including for example the capture of Jerusalem by the Romans and the atrocities that then occurred;

    d. Symbolic representations concerning the religious life, such as Mary the Mother of God shown sitting in a garden, as a symbol of the Immaculate Conception. When Mary is portrayed with a unicorn, this animal also represents Christ. Sometimes the scene is completed by other figures, of whom for example a hunter represents the Archangel Gabriel, and the hounds bear names such as Peace, Justice, Mercy, etc.;

    e. tapestries relating to the Creed, on which prophets and apostles, as representatives of the Old and the New Testaments, are often placed face to face;

    f. stories from the New Testament;

g. scenes from the Apocalypse.

VII. Allegories
Allegories on life in general.
Allegories on temperance and intemperance.
Representations of the virtues and vices:
    a. the so-called theological virtues: Hope, Faith and Charity;
    b. the cardinal virtues: Strength, Righteousness, Temperance
    and Courage;
    c. the deadly sins: Pride, Envy, Lust, Avarice, Gluttony, Sloth,
    etc.
These vices were represented in different ways, usually in
connection with some animal that illustrates the vice. Thus the
he-goat stood for lust, the wolf for greed, the dragon for avarice,
the bear for unchastity, etc.
The battle between these virtues and vices was often depicted
in the form of a tournament.

VIII. Representations relating to Chivalry
Tourneys.
Hunting-tapestries, often combined with religious ideas.
Armorial tapestries.
Tapestries to do with courtly love:
    a. the fountain of love;
    b. the fountain of eternal youth.

IX. Other subjects
Fables.
Professions.
Verdures.

In the Sixteenth Century
Many of the themes current in the previous centuries maintained their interest. These we shall not mention again in this
section, but limit ourselves to stating a few subjects that came
to the fore in this century. The list makes no claim to be complete.

I. Relating to ancient history and mythology
The story of Erysichthon, who, among other things, sold his
daughter to appease his perpetual hunger.

The story of Perseus.

The story of Vertumnus and Pomona, according to Ovid's Metamorphoses.

Other subjects borrowed from Ovid:

    a. the rescue of Andromeda;

    b. the punishment of Marsyas;

    c. the fall of Icarus;

    d. the abduction of Ganymede;

    e. the sacrifice of Polyxena;

    f. the love of Mars and Venus.

The story of Danaë.

The story of Psyche.

Stories of historical personages were also much in demand, among others that of King Cyrus.

The heroic tapestries were also still being made, depicting, for example, the Trojan heroes.

II. *Relating to contemporary events*

The most famous series is that which the Emperor Charles V had made, concerning his wars. Of these we shall name:

    a. the capture of Tunis in 1535;

    b. the battle of Pavia.

Other well-known tapestries to do with happenings of the time form part of a series celebrating the deeds of the Duke of Alva; the battle of Jemmingen where Louis of Nassau, a brother of William of Orange, met his death belongs to this group.

III. *Religious subjects*

At this time, these mostly related to parallels drawn between the Old and the New Testaments, and were borrowed from woodcuts appearing in the *Biblia Pauperum*, the Bible of the Poor, that originated in the beginning of the fourteenth century. The subjects to which these parallels generally related, and allusions to which we find already in the liturgical prayers of the early Christians, include the following:

    a. the preaching of the Gospel: Eve and the serpent; also Gideon and his fleece;

    b. the nativity: Moses and the burning bush; also the rod of Aaron putting forth flowers;

    c. the slaughter of the innocents: Saul smiting the priestly city of Nob; also Queen Athaliah letting her family perish;

    d. the temptation of Christ in the wilderness: the Fall; also Esau selling his birthright;

e. the raising of Lazarus: Elijah raising the widow's son; also Elijah raising a child from the dead;

f. the entry of Jesus into Jerusalem: David with the head of Goliath; also the prophet Elisha receiving the mantle of Elijah;

g. the Last Supper: the meeting of Abraham and Melchizedek, king of Salem; also the dew of manna in the wilderness;

h. the bearing of the Cross: Isaac carrying wood for his own sacrifice; also the widow of Sarepta;

i. Christ on the Cross: the sacrifice that God asked of Abraham; also the brazen serpent in the wilderness;

j. Christ's entombment: Joseph in the pit or Jonah in the whale;

k. the Resurrection: Samson bearing away the Gates of Gaza, or Jonah being cast out on dry land by the fish;

l. the Ascension: either Enoch or Elijah being carried up into heaven;

m. the coming of the Holy Ghost: Moses receiving the Law; also the consuming of Elijah's sacrifice;

n. the coronation of Mary: King Solomon setting his mother beside him on his throne, or Esther finding favour with King Ahasuerus.

The life of Mary.

The Passion of Christ.

The Creed. On these tapestries the Holy Trinity is often represented. This was rendered in the following ways:

a. On the divine throne sit three persons wearing the imperial crown, sceptre and mantle. Round the throne we see the Seraphim, the Cherubim, the Thrones, the Dominions, the Virtues, the Powers, the Princes, the Archangels and the Angels. Before the throne appear Justice and Truth, accusing mankind, and Mercy and Peace, pleading for mankind. This is the oldest form, which appeared as early as the fourteenth century;

b. God the Father is portrayed as an ancient, the Son as a man in his prime, and the Holy Ghost as a youth;

c. God the Father and the Son are seen enthroned, while the Holy Ghost flies above them in the form of a dove.

The Acts of the Apostles.

The Last Supper.

The Triumph of Christ.

The parables of Jesus, of which we shall only mention:

a. the Prodigal Son;

b. the Good Samaritan;

c. Lazarus and the rich man;

d. the wise and foolish virgins.

101

IV. Allegories

Now we come to those tapestries with allegorical figures representing stars and planets. In the middle, the influence of the planet on human life is often depicted; in the four corners its effect on health in particular. They bear an astrological character, wholly in keeping with the spirit of the time, and thus were indispensable for those who valued health and prosperity. These tapestries appeared as early as the fifteenth century. In this connection, we should also mention the 'Lucas' Months, a set of tapestries after sixteenth century designs by a painter whose Christian name alone is known. On these tapestries the planets are shown as allegorical figures riding in a triumphal car. Among them we find:

a. Saturn: the god of agriculture, and thus the patron of bakers, farmers, and of justice. Under his dominion falls the month of January, with its sign of Aquarius the Water-Carrier, as well as February, with that of Pisces, the Fishes;

b. Jupiter: god of the chase and patron of scholars, judges, and, among others, workers in the textile trade. Under his dominion fall March, with the sign of Aries the Ram, and April with that of Taurus the Bull;

c. Mars: god of war and patron of butchers. Months: May (Gemini the Twins) and June (Cancer the Crab);

d. Apollo: god of the sun and of the harvest. Month: July, Leo the Lion;

e. Venus: goddess of love, and patron of artists, weavers, dyers, embroiderers and musicians. Months: August (the Virgin) and September (Libra, the Scales);

f. Mercury: god of physicians and patron of money-changers, painters, sculptors, organ-builders and clock-makers. Months: October (the Scorpion) and November (the Archer);

g. Luna: goddess of home industry, sport, etc. Month: December (Capricorn the Goat).

Equally, if not more popular, were the allegorical Triumphs of Petrarch:

a. the triumph of chastity over love;

b. the triumph of death over chastity;

c. the triumph of time over death;

d. the triumph of fame over time.

Many allegories were also applied to point a moral. The ruinous practice of gambling was symbolised, as were unbridled lust and vanity. The series could be extended indefinitely.

V. Ancestor-Tapestries

Personal glorification at this time had become much less devious than formerly, and the princes of the various houses eagerly sought to extol the real or fancied deeds of their illustrious forebears. The Swedes, the Danes, the Portugese, the Spanish princes of Aragon and Castile, all had their ancestors depicted in the tapestries. Most of the reigning houses followed their example.

VI. Hunting-Tapestries

These held their ground as a class, but now they had come furnished with all kinds of wild animals – a direct consequence of the suddenly-arisen fashion for keeping a collection of wild animals in the castle grounds. These animals soon found a place in the garden-tapestries, as well, which represented the Late Middle Ages parks around the castles of the high nobility.

These tapestries have a background covered with thousands of flowers. The 'mille-fleur' tapestries were to live on, with many variations, in the 'verdures'.

VII. Scenes from the Old Testament

The story of Noah – extremely popular, because all those animals could play their part!
The story of David and Bathsheba.

VIII. Other Subjects

Here should be mentioned tapestries with scenes of the dance – the so-called Moresque tapestries – which bring pastoral adventures, love-games, and eventually even children's games, into the tapestries. Armorial tapestries remained in demand.

In the Seventeenth Century

I. Relating to ancient history and mythology

The classics continued to provide material. We shall mention only:
The story of Diana (Ovid).
The stories of Theseus, Romulus, Pompey, Alexander, Julius Caesar and Mark Antony (Plutarch).
The story of Alexander the Great, yet again (Quintus Curtius Rufus).
The story of Philippus (Justinian).

The history of the Roman people (Eutropius and Livy).

II. Contemporary Events
The destruction of the Armada.
The battle of Zierikzee.
The battle of Rammekens, etc.
The coronation of King Louis XIII. This tapestry is one of the celebrated 'Grands chevaux' series.
The visit of King Louis XIV to the Gobelin factory in Paris.
Cardinal Chigi being received in audience by Louis XIV.
The meeting between Louis XIV and Philip IV of Spain.
Louis XIV's entry into Dunkirk, etc.

III. Hero-Worship
The epic poem *Orlando Furioso* by Ludovici Ariosto, in which many heroes of times gone by are described, was the starting point for various renowned tapestry sequences. Twenty different imitations were made.

IV. The Pastoral Tapestry
The tapestry with pastoral scenes was very popular in this century. After the *Orlando* mentioned above, which also supplied material for these pastorals, the *Aminta* of Torquato Tasso and *Il Pastor Fido* of Guarini likewise provided favoured subjects. The *Diana* of Georg de Monmayor and the *Galatea* of Cervantes can also be named.

V. Allegories
In this century we may distinguish according to their subjects, allegories on love; the ailments to which man is exposed; the calumnies to which he falls a victim; on the church and the creed and everything connected with them; on heroic deeds; the virtues; and so forth.
Concerning religion, we shall only mention here the series designed by Rubens: the Triumph of the Eucharist.
Of the heroic tapestries, the sequences concerning the life of Constantine and the life of Decius Mus.
Among these allegorical tapestries we may also count those which derived from the ballet performances and particularly from the entr'actes. Here certain episodes were enacted, which reappeared time and again in the tapestries, such as, for example: Saturn being bound by *amoretti;*
Putti robbing Mars of his weapons, etc.

104

Numerous also were the tapestries depicting proverbs and fables, which may also be included in this group.

VI. *Hunting-Tapestries*
These still remained popular, although it is evident the quarry more and more existed only in the fantasy of the designers.

VII. *Religious representations*
These were made much less often than in former times, but certain stories, such as that of Moses, continued on the looms, because they gave occasion for portraying magnificent country-life scenes – extremely popular at the time.

VIII. *Other Subjects*
Country-life, with peasants dancing, or smoking or eating, stood at the focus of interest.
In the armorial tapestries, an allegorical figure frequently took the place of the arms, at this period.

In the Eighteenth Century
I. *Relating to ancient history and mythology*
The classics continued to furnish material, but the number of subjects declined.

II. *Contemporary Themes*
The subjects chosen became continually more trivial.

III. *Allegories*
Interest in this sort of subject declined rapidly, along with the sense of the symbolic.

IV. *The Pastoral Tapestry*
This steadily gained preference over all other subjects.

V. *Other Subjects*
As such we may mention:
  a. work on the land;
  b. the adventures of Don Quixote;
  c. the 'Burlesque', with figures from the Italian comedy.

Bibliography

Books

Schmitz H., Bildteppiche (Berlin, 1921)
Göbel H., Wandteppiche, 3 vols (Leipzig, 1923–1934)
Dermotte J., La Tapisserie gothique (Paris, 1923)
Kurth B., Gotische Bildteppiche aus Frankreich und Flandern (Munich, 1923)
—, Die Deutschen Bildteppiche des Mittelalters, 3 vols (Vienna, 1926)
Cassou J., M. Damain et R. Moutard-Uldry, La Tapisserie Française et les Peintres cartonniers (Paris, 1957)
Gatti-Garinni G., L'Arazzo (Florence, 1958)
Blazkova J., La Tapisserie des collections Tchecosloveques (Paris, 1958)
Guimbaud L., La Tapisserie de haute- et basse-lisse (Paris, 1959)
Lanz J., Tapisseries Gothiques (Lausanne, 1959)
Weigert R. A., La Tapisserie Française (Paris, 1956) [English translation by D. and M. King, London, 1962]
Ysselstein G. T. van, Geschiedenis der tapijtweverijen in de Noordelijke Nederlanden (Leiden, 1936)
Thomson W. G., A History of Tapestry (London, 1930) [Revised edition]
Thomson W. G., Tapestry Weaving in England (London, 1914)
Marillier H. C., English Tapestries of the 18th century (London, 1930)
Fischer E. and G. Ingers, Flamskvävnad (Malmö, 1961)
Heinz D., Europäische Wandteppiche, I (Brunswick, 1963)

Magazine Articles

Kalf J., Alexander Baert, Tapestry-Maker. Amsterdamsch Jaarboekje (1904)
Göbel H., Holländische Wandteppich Manufakturen. Der Cicerone XIV (1922)
Schelven A. A. van, Nederlandsche wandtapijtweverijen in het Engeland van de zeventiende eeuw. Oud-Holland (1925)
Kalf E. J., Drie Leyniers-tapijten te Middelburg. Artes Textiles (1959–1960)

Museums

Most of the larger museums publish beautifully-illustrated catalogues on this subject. We only mention:
Urseau Ch., Le Musée des Tapisseries d'Angers (Paris, 1930)
Planchenault R., Les Tapisseries d'Angers (Paris)

106

Magazines

Artes Textiles. Contributions to the history of the art of tapestry, embroidery and textiles. Publishing centre for the history of the textile arts, Blandijnberg, 2, Ghent, Belgium.

Museums

Museums in the United States having collections of tapestries

Albany, New York: Albany Institute of History and Art
Baltimore, Maryland: Baltimore Museum of Art
Baltimore, Maryland: Walters Art Gallery
Boston, Massachusetts: Isabella Stewart Gardner Museum
Boston, Massachusetts: Museum of Fine Arts
Cincinnati, Ohio: Cincinnati Art Museum
Detroit, Michigan: The Detroit Institute of Arts
Hartford, Connecticut: Wadsworth Atheneum
Los Angeles, California: Los Angeles County Museum
Louisville, Kentucky: J. B. Speed Art Museum
Minneapolis, Minnesota: Minneapolis Institute of Arts
New York, New York: The Metropolitan Museum of Art (The Cloisters)
Portland, Maine: Portland Museum of Art
Richmond, Virginia: Virginia Museum of Fine Arts
Rochester, New York: Rochester Memorial Art Gallery
San Francisco, California: California Palace of the Legion of Honor
San Francisco, California: M. H. de Young Memorial Museum
Washington, D.C.: Corcoran Gallery of Art
Washington, D.C.: National Gallery of Art
Worcester, Massachusetts: Worcester Art Museum

Collections of tapestries in Great Britain

Most of the City Museums have one or two tapestries in their galleries of decorative arts. Worth mentioning separately are:

The Bowes Museum, Barnard Castle
Belfast, Ulster Museum

The only large collections are at:

The Victoria and Albert Museum, London
The Burrell Collection, Glasgow, which is at present partly shown in the Kelvingrove Art Gallery and Museum.

Most of the tapestries in Great Britain are to be seen in the houses and palaces open to the public, administered by the Ministry of Works, the National Trust, and private owners. The collections at:

Hampton Court Palace and
Hardwick Hall, Derbyshire

are perhaps the most important. Tapestries can also be seen at:

Cliveden, Bucks.
Denham Place, Denham, Bucks.
Waddesdon Manor, Bucks.
Sawston Hall, Cambridge.
Bramhall Hall, Cheshire
Lyme Park, Cheshire
Cotehele, Cornwall
Forde Abbey, Nr. Chard, Dorset
Berkeley Castle, Gloucs.
Eastnor Castle, Herefordshire.
Hatfield House, Herts.
Squerryes Court, Westerham, Kent.
Astley Hall, Chorley, Lancs.
Browsholme Hall, Chorley, Lancs.
Hinwick House, Nr. Wellingborough, Northants.
Castle Ashby, Northants.
Burghley House, Northants.
Stapleford Park, Nr. Melton Mowbray, Leicestershire
Belvoir Castle, Nr. Grantham
Montacute House, Yeovil, Somerset.
Newby Hall, Ripon, Yorks.

Powis Castle, Welshpool, Montgomeryshire
Chirk Castle, Nr. Wrexham.

Bantry House, Bantry, Co. Cork.

Photographs

Black-and-white photographs:

1 a and b. Atelier de la Savonnerie.
1c. Atelier de Beauvais Basse Lisse.
2a. A.C.L., Brussels.
2c up to and including 16. Crown C.R., London.

Colour plates:

I *a, b and c.* W. and B. Forman (Artia, Prague).
II *a and b.* F. Ili Pedrotti, Trento.
III *a and b.* Armand Colin-Veronèse.
IV *a and b.* Publication Filmées d'Art et d'Histoire.

Explanation of the Cover:

The tapestry on the cover forms part of a series known as the *Triumphs of Petrarch*. A beautiful example of similar 'triumphs' which had long been extremely popular, this tapestry represents the triumph of Fame, who is seen standing in a chariot drawn by elephants, on the righthand side. On the left, another chariot is depicted – the triumphal car of the Fates, on which lies Chastity, in bonds. One of the Fates – Atropos, 'she who cannot be avoided' – stands at her head, but is being thrust down from her dominating position by Fame. This she does by sounding her trumpet, a noise that can even bring the dead to life. The other Fates, Clotho and Lachesis, are being crushed beneath the chariot wheels.

The mingling of classical and Christian allusions, which the designers delighted to employ in order to honour their powerful clients, is clearly to be observed in this tapestry. Thus, among others, we see Julius Caesar – in the costume of the sixteenth century, of course – awarded a place of honour in the procession. The arms on his tunic, nevertheless, display the eagle of the Hapsburg family, and the Burgundian arms likewise make their appearance in the tapestry. Sufficient grounds, surely, for concluding that the series to which this tapestry belongs must have had some connection with these families, or perhaps even had been commissioned by them.

This tapestry was woven in Brussels in the first quarter of the sixteenth century, and is now in the possession of the Rijksmuseum at Amsterdam.

109

Drawings

By the author:
Fig. 1 – after Göbel* pl. 23
Fig. 2 – after Göbel pl. 5, see also Diderot** pl. IX
Fig. 3   after Göbel pl. 8, see also Diderot pl. XIII
Fig. 4 – after Göbel pl. 8, see also Diderot pl. XIII
Fig. 5 – after Göbel pl. 9, 10, 11, see also Diderot pl. X
Fig. 6 – after Göbel pl. 8, see also Diderot pl. XIII
Fig. 7 – after Göbel pl. 25
Fig. 9 – after Göbel pl. 31
Fig. 10 – after Göbel pl. 29
Fig. 11 – after Göbel pl. 27, 27a
Fig. 17 – after Göbel pl. 5, see also Diderot pl. IX
Fig. 18 – after Göbel pl. 19, see also Diderot pl. XVIII
Fig. 19
Fig. 20
Fig. 21 – after Louis de Farcy
Fig. 22

By Freek Visser:
Fig. 8 – after Göbel pl. 39
Fig. 12
Fig. 13
Fig. 14
Fig. 15
Fig. 16

By Pieter Pouwels:
Fig. 23
Fig. 24
Fig. 25
Fig. 26
Fig. 27

* H. Göbel, Die Wandteppiche Teil I, Die Niederlande Band I.
** Diderot, Encyclopédie des Arts et Métiers, Paris 1751–1772, supplément 1776–1777. Chapters Tapisserie de Basse-lisse, Tapisserie de Haute-lisse, Registre 1780.